THE IDEAL PENTECOSTAL CHURCH

BY

SETH C. REES

"Christ also loved the church, and gave himself for it; that he might sanctify and cleanse it with the washing of water by the word, that he might present it to himself a glorious church, not having spot or wrinkle, or any such thing; but that it should be holy and without blemish."

—Eph. v. 25-27.

CINCINNATI, O.

THE REVIVALIST OFFICE.

DEDICATION.

IN loving dedication to the wife of my youth, who for twenty years has been my greatest earthly blessing, and who still abides with me amidst the sorrows and joys, trials and triumphs of a conquering Christian life.

Bert Holcomb

Westport

Ind

Lena Holcombs' Book.

~~Trusting~~ He will make it a great blessing to your soul!.

Yours & His
Seth C. Rees

CONTENTS.

INTRODUCTION.

In these "last days," when "perilous times" are upon us, we do well to take our bearings and, with chart in hand, ascertain our spiritual latitude and longitude. To all who read the signs of the times it is evident that the so-called church is not the "powerful church" God intended her to be. The supernatural is no longer expected or desired. Worldliness is displayed in buildings, forms of worship and financial methods. Formality, coldness, stagnation and decay, mark many modern churches. All who devoutly pray for a Holy Ghost awakening will rejoice that there is added to our literature so clear and terse a work as "The Ideal Pentecostal Church." It is a treatise on the characteristics and qualities of the Pentecostal Church, *i. e.*, that part of the Church which has received her Pentecost. Our author writes not as a theorist but as one who, having received the baptism with the Holy Ghost and fire, has proven himself "a workman that needeth not to be ashamed," and has witnessed under his own ministry the striking characteristics of a Pentecostal Church. In putting this work before the public he seeks only the glory of God. May the Holy Spirit use these pages to awaken a slumbering Church to her perils and her privileges.

JOHN PENNINGTON.

MT. PLEASANT, OHIO, March 20, 1897.

THE IDEAL PENTECOSTAL CHURCH.

CHAPTER I.

OPENING CHAPTER.

For at least six thousand years God has had his idea of what the Pentecostal Church should be. From the time he first viewed the wreck and ruin of the race, wrought by that miracle of hell, sin, he knew what was possible for Him to bring out of the *debris*. Just as a sculptor, before ever he touches the marble with chisel or mallet, has a clear conception of his statue; just as a painter sees his picture long before the brush begins to transform the face of the canvas; just as the architect conceives of his building in his mind, while as yet not a line has been drawn nor a stroke of work accomplished; so God saw from the first the possibilities of grace in the Church, the Bride, the Lamb's wife.

Every pure and true man has his idea of what he desires to find in the woman who is to be his wife. Like the needle to the pole, her heart must be true to her husband. She must not flirt with other men nor cast adulterous glances at old lovers. Separated from all others, she must be loyal to him. No noble man will ever bear to the old homestead, to father and mother and loved ones, a wife whom he even suspicions as unworthy. She must not only be pure and true herself, but she must be capable of entering fully into the secrets of his life, of sharing his sorrows as well as his joys, of sympathizing with him, both in his sufferings and in his triumphs.

So Christ had his idea of what he would like to have as a bride. He has most emphatically expressed his wishes concerning the character of the wife who is to be his companion throughout eternity. Splendid preparations are now being made for the celebration of the nuptials; and she, whom the spotless Christ bears on his arm into the royal halls of glory, must fill his idea.

If we can know God's opinion, if we can find out his thought concerning any matter, it is of no consequence to us what churches think or what creeds say. It makes no difference about the jargon of the schools. From the "Thus saith the Lord" there can be no appeal. God has not left us in the dark as to what his thought for the church is. He has taken every pains to give us a clear understanding of Christ's wishes and desires in the matter; and whatever Christ has desired to see in his church, his bride, is made gloriously attainable and possible through the power of the cross.

In the second chapter of the Acts of the Apostles we find plainly enunciated the characteristics of the "Ideal Pentecostal Church." May the dear Holy Spirit anoint our eyes to see the truth as it is set forth in this Scripture.

CHAPTER II.

OF WHOM COMPOSED.

The Ideal Pentecostal Church is composed of regenerated souls. There is not an unconverted person in all its membership. Moreover, God's definition of regeneration differs from that of man. It means more by fearful odds than is popularly supposed for a man to be Scripturally regenerated. The New Testament type of spiritual birth does not come about by the mere raising of the hand, the signing of a card, the donning of a badge, the submitting to ordinances, or the joining of a society called a "church."

BIBLE regeneration is preceded by deep and pungent conviction for sin, and a repentance that unhesitatingly renounces the "world, the flesh, and the devil." It regulates all the irregularities of outward life. If we had more old-fashioned conviction, followed by old-fashioned conversion, resulting in old-time shouting, we would have far more candidates for the baptism with the Holy Ghost.

But this is an age of compromise, and the baneful results are seen in the nature of the converts produced. An ease-loving, pleasure-seeking, time-serving, compromising church does not, and can not, turn out healthy converts. A good start is valuable in anything; and it is eminently true in Christianity. The one hundred and twenty had been converted, either under the ministry of that inflexible preacher of righteousness, John the Baptist, or else under the teaching of Christ himself. Jesus said that they were branches of the true Vine. He admonished them to rejoice that their "names were written in heaven," and in his great sacerdotal prayer, he tells the Father that they are not of the world, even as he is not of the world. These men had forsaken their nets and followed Christ, and when "the day of Pentecost was fully come" it found them pursuing a manner of life in which "they were continually in the temple blessing and praising God." They hugged reproach and loosened their hold on earthly things.

Regeneration is a conscious experience. They who are regenerated KNOW IT. If we are not assured of our regeneration, no one knows it to be a fact, not even God himself. If we are not fully aware that we are born from above, it is not a fact, and a preacher's saying so will not make it true. The witness of the Holy Spirit will let us know it, when we are really regenerated; and so satisfactory is this "witness" to him who receives it that he would not thank a committee from the upper skies to appear and confirm it.

Regeneration is replete with joy, with warm religious feeling, and with real fervency of spirit. Indeed, it usually produces more of these heavenly graces than many possess who *claim* entire sanctification. There is a great lack of warmth, glow, and holy emotion in the religious world to-day. The emotional element in salvation is by no means a small one. "The kingdom of God is righteousness, joy and peace in the Holy Ghost." Joy and peace are both feeling. Thousands say that they have taken Christ by faith, but that they have never had a clear witness of the Spirit to their pardon. What a farce! Much of our teaching about "taking it by faith" and "holding on by faith," *et cetera*, is responsible for this deplorable state of affairs. Beloved, faith has a bit of evidence in it, and real genuine faith gets an answer. Faith is the means by which we get all our blessings and, when genuine, is always honored by the witness of the Spirit.

Regeneration brings us resurrection life. We no longer plod toward the grave, but have turned our backs on the sepulchre and are speeding toward Galilee with a glad message for the disciples. Many, burdened with spices to embalm their Lord, with sad, sorrow-stricken faces, crawl dismally toward the tomb, forgetting that Christ has risen from the dead. One throb of his pulse was sufficient to burst asunder the bands of death, break the waxen seal, throw open the sepulchre door, and stun and paralyze the sturdy Roman guard. And with Him, we also, in the power of His resurrection life, step out from the dark tomb and climb upon the casket of our old life in glorious, gladsome triumph. Many are busily attempting to embalm Christianity. The churches, in so far as they are merely sects or societies, may be embalmed and, alas, many of them are, reminding us of Egyptian mummies, sleeping peacefully in their several sarcophagi, opened to view only on state occasions. Expert undertakers tell us that the chemicals positively refuse to act so long as there remains the slightest particle of life. Thank God, a living Christian can not be embalmed. The antiseptics of the world do not affect a living church in the slightest. This poor world is dying for the want of men and women who will go and publish the fact that Jesus has risen from the dead and is alive for evermore. The cross and the sepulchre, when viewed from certain standpoints, are bleak and dark and cold. Most of the professors of religion stand on the north side of the cross, full in its dark, gloomy shadow, chilled to the marrow, and almost dead. But, blessed be God, there is a south side, genial, warm, sunny and bright. It is the place of spring-time. Flowers leap up from the ground; the birds sing overhead; and fountains of sparkling, living, inexhaustible water play in abundance.

> "I've reached the land of Beulah,
> The summer-land of love,
> Land of the heavenly Bridegroom,
> Land of the Holy Dove;
> My winter has departed,
> My summer-time has come,
> The air is full of singing,
> The earth is bright with bloom."

CHAPTER III.

A CLEAN CHURCH.

"Purifying their hearts by faith" (Acts xv. 9). Holiness is a state; entire sanctification is an experience; the Holy Ghost is a person. We come into the state of holiness through the experience of entire sanctification, wrought by the omnipotent energies of the Holy Ghost. This is the "baptism with the Holy Ghost and fire" administered by Christ himself, as John the Baptist declares. He did not mean that there were two baptisms, one with the Spirit and another with fire, but *one* "baptism with the Holy Ghost" under the *symbol* of fire.

There are some things which the application of water will not cleanse. Water may cleanse the loose dirt on the outside, but fire alone can make inwardly, intrinsically clean. Metal ore is not refined by mere washing—it must undergo the crushing and smelting processes. Again and again the base ore is subjected to the fiery ordeal, until every iota of the useless grit and undesirable sand is destroyed and the metal is left free from alloy. So the water of regeneration will free the soul from external sin-commission, but the sanctifying process of the Spirit is requisite if the heart is to be holy and sinless.

Poisonous air may be driven from old wells and mine-shafts with fire. The deadly gases must yield before the flame. And the fire of the Spirit will rout all miasma and malaria from both pulpit and pew.

Nothing is more refreshing on a hot, sultry July afternoon than a thunder-storm. A few vivid flashes, a half-dozen dashes of blinding flame, and lo, the atmosphere has become bracing and invigorating. Of all urgent needs, none is more truly evident than that the church ought to be struck with double-geared lightning from the upper skies. The jagged bolts should be allowed to play on both preacher and people. This celestial electricity would sweeten the spiritual atmosphere in our churches and in our own souls. It would burn away all the fog of uncertainty and unbelief and doubt, and give us convictions born of assurance.

Proud flesh requires the fire. Nothing rivals it in the dispatch and effectiveness with which it does its work. A Boston physician told me that, with all the modern discoveries of science, there had been nothing found that would do but fire. In the moral world there is nothing obtainable that will cure proud flesh in our natures and in our churches except Pentecostal fire. This alone will kill the "brag," the pomp, the gusto, the ungodly strut so evident in so many professors of religion to-day. Let us take down our lightning rods, all our preventatives, and fire, celestial fire, will leap over the battlements of heaven and fall upon us, slaying all our pride, destroying all our tin, dross, and reprobate silver, and giving us a joyous release from all chaff and from all that is light-weight.

Those who have received their Pentecost live pure, holy lives. They never practice unclean habits, whether secret or known. They do not have unclean thoughts, unchaste desires, or unholy passions. They do not use wine, beer, tobacco, snuff or opium. True, a man may have his name on a church-book and yet indulge in these things of which we speak; but he might just as well have it on a board fence, for it does not make him a member of the Pentecostal company. He may "belong to the meeting-house," but he is not one of this blessed fire-crowned throng.

Men who are in unholy connection with this Godless world in lodges, fraternities and Christless institutions, or who will stoop to the commercial trickeries of this age, or who will lend their influence to abet a questionable business, have not been through the furnace of the upper room. Pentecostal Christians have "clean hands and pure hearts." "Hands" in the Bible refers to the outward, manifest, visible life. It refers to what man sees. The word has regard to *conduct*. The life must be clean. A man can not be in close contact with the world without being contaminated. Lot well nigh became a Sodomite by dwelling in Sodom and among Sodom's inhabitants; and intimate relationship with men of unrighteous lives always means demoralization for the Christian. "Clean hands" hold no bribes, they never deal unjustly, they do not give thirty-five inches for a yard nor fifteen ounces for a pound, they do not pay debts at forty cents on the dollar when they could do more.

The behavior of the tongue is included in the life. The conversation must be pure and chaste, never vulgar, never immodest. The jest with its indelicate association is never heard on the mouth of the Pentecostal saint.

The phrase "clean heart" relates to the inward, invisible, secret nature—that which God alone sees. It describes a condition of things in which there is no pride, or anger, or jealousy, or envy, or strife, or selfishness, or worldly ambition, or *any* unholy temper. Desire for place or position in church or state is purged away. We who are of the Pentecostal Church see no one who has a place we would desire. We are not wire-pulling to get a position. We are saved from political scheming in ecclesiastical circles, as well as elsewhere. In honor we prefer one another. There can be no anxiety, for God makes all our appointments for us.

When the heart is clean the Holy Ghost saves us from all peevishness, fretfulness, sensitiveness and touchiness. We hardly know when we are insulted and, therefore, never take offense. As Dr. Carradine says, we get so we "can *live* on cold shoulder and cold tongue." We are not looking out for slights. If any one pays any attention to us, it is that much more than we deserve, that much clear gain.

How plainly uncleanness of heart reveals itself in the actions, tempers and ambitions of the disciples previous to their Pentecost! They were selfish: they wanted the best places. Instance John and James bidding for chief seats. Notice the anger and indignation consequent upon the rest of the twelve hearing of the request of the two brothers. But, passing the upper room experience, we look in vain to find evidences of envy or self-seeking in these men. That Pentecostal electrocution forever put an end to the self-life.

How this fiery cleansing would relieve the church to-day! Office-seeking preachers would not buttonhole the bishops. This continual lobbying of which the presiding elder or superintendent is the unhappy subject would cease. Men would be more anxious to show their devotion to Christ and self-denial for his cause, than to obtain the best appointments. An unheard-of thing might possibly be, *viz.*, a vacancy on the official board, and no one sitting up nights concocting a scheme which would lift him to the place.

Would-be generals are abundant nowadays. There are plenty of men who would gladly boss God's army. They want to be bell-sheep. *They* must tinkle the bell, and no one else. If they can't be bell-sheep, they won't be sheep at all, but turn goats. Certainly we need the holy flame to extirpate unholy ambitions.

Before Pentecost, the disciples were sectarian. One poor fellow was having a glorious time casting out devils. "Does he follow us?" "No." "Forbid him. Stop the revival; complain to the authorities! Schism! Tendency to divide! Comeoutism!" There are thousands of people who have no sympathy with a work, however praiseworthy, without the movers in that work are in full unison with them on all points.

A revengeful spirit crops out in the pre-Pentecostal disciples. "Opposition?" "Down with fire!" "Do not like to hear us preach?" "Rain brimstone!" This is the un-Christlike spirit of even some *so called* Holiness preachers. "We can't punish you, but God can. We will get the Lord to revenge us." How different is the meekness, the heart-lowliness of the Son of God. "Despised" and "rejected," "yet he opened not his mouth." Vengeance and retaliation are burned out of us when we are sanctified, and unholy resentment thereafter finds in the soul no place.

CHAPTER IV.

A POWERFUL CHURCH.

"Ye shall receive power after that the Holy Ghost is come upon you." There can be no success without power. Power is the very condition of success. It is the all-important need of the people of God, for by its presence failure is placed beyond the range of possibility. The word translated in our Authorized Version as "power" is the word from which the term "dynamite" is taken. Indeed, no violence whatsoever is done to the text if we read: "Ye shall receive *dynamite* after that the Holy Ghost is come upon you." "Behold I have given you *dynamite* above all the *dynamite* of the enemy." Thus we see that Pentecostal power is, in the spiritual world, what dynamite is in the material. Consider its explosive, overturning effects in the ministry of the Apostles. "These that have turned the world upside down have come hither also." To the carnally minded, the world appears right side up though in reality it is upside down, and in need of the reversive dynamite of the Holy Ghost.

This power is promised to us, and with it success

is sure. Not only is its possession a privilege, but a positive duty. We are as certainly commanded to "be strong in the Lord and in the power of his might" as we are commanded not to steal. It would, therefore, be just as proper for you, a Christian, to get up in class- or testimony-meeting, and talk about your tendency to steal, to lust, or to lie, as to talk about your "weakness," "shortcomings," "crooked paths," or "feeble remarks." Weakness is a spreading malady. Strength is a spreading energy. I can not afford to be weak, for it is not merely a misfortune to fail—it is a *crime* in the sight of high heaven.

If a man may be as strong financially as his financial backing, why may we not be as strong spiritually as our spiritual backing? We ought never to *think* of failing until the resources of heaven are completely exhausted. We should make no arrangements for defeat until we are certain that heaven is bankrupt. If we are cabled to the throne we may expect to fall only when the white throne itself crumbles, totters and goes down. Glory! Most of Christians are looking out for a soft place to fall. They make preparations to tumble. They are like the sister who said she could "never give up the blessed old doctrine of falling from grace." They believe so thoroughly in backsliding that they indulge in it frequently.

No one says that it is impossible to backslide; but certainly it is not necessary to sin. We are not preaching impeccability, but we are magnifying the grace of God in its ability and power to save from sin and make the human heart victorious. "All things are possible with God" and "All things are possible to him that believeth." Faith is the alchemy which changes fear to courage, "crooked paths" to king's highways, and "feeble efforts" to glorious "exploits." If we fear a fear it will come upon us. He who indulges in talk about "crooked paths" will have plenty of "crooked paths" to talk about. He who refers to his public communications as "feeble remarks" in general describes the true nature of what he says; if he *thinks* they are "feeble," they *are* "feeble," so great is the importance of faith. If a man has a message from God and delivers it "with the Holy Ghost sent down from heaven" he will have no occasion to speak of his ministry as an "effort" or "endeavor." Mere endeavorers do nothing but endeavor, and are satisfied with simply endeavoring. They do not talk of success. Victory is not expected. They anticipate but little, and are never disappointed.

Let us repeat: The Pentecostal Church is a *powerful* church. This power is not the power of numbers. Israel was often weakest as a matter of fact when she numbered the most; while Gideon's three hundred were more mighty than his thirty-two thousand. Many a church of six hundred members is filled with pygmies, dwarfs, and stunted babies. "New-born babes desiring the sincere milk of the Word" they have not, neither would they know what to do with them if they had them, for they have not had a convert in five years. These stunted weaklings are "whiney," finicky, hard to please; they must be petted and coddled and put up in scented cotton, requiring the nursing of two hard-working pastors continually.

Many a church-society with a large membership is struggling along, scarcely maintaining an existence, using almost every questionable means to eke out the money necessary to keep the thing going, while some little Holiness mission with no earthly backing whatsoever is having hundreds of souls saved. We know a small Holiness mission in New York City which averaged one hundred and thirty-five converts a month. Thus we see God is not so particular about quantity as he is about quality. Israel always made a mistake when she began to consider numbers and enumerate the people. *God* was all she needed. The tendency of all ages is to count noses and trust in a crowd. The effort to-day is to make a greater *showing*. Ministers make a grave mistake in bending every energy to increase the membership; we need to stop and clean up what we have. We may carry the report of large numbers to Conference or our annual gatherings, but when the judgment day has cut our bloated statistics down to the real count we may be unable to recognize our congregations. We would rather have a dozen men and women separated from the world and filled with condensed lightning from the upper skies than to have a huge convocation of time-serving ecclesiastics. The writer knows men who have been fished out of the slums, saved, wholly sanctified, healed, and charged with chain-lightning until he would rather have them sit near the pulpit and pray while he preaches than to be backed by a whole bench of bishops.

Again, the power of the ideal Pentecostal Church is not that of intellect or brains. We are told that knowledge is power, and yet many who stuff their heads and starve their hearts grow weaker every day. This power of which we speak is not the product of seminaries, colleges and universities. It does not come by metaphysical research or philosophical reflection. The ancient Greeks were cultured and oftentimes refined, but utterly destitute of this power. The musty records of the Chinese show a keen appreciation of scientific methods and brains fertile in the production of philosophies, yet the Celestials, even in the palmy days of Confucius, knew nothing of this power.

Corinth, noted for her rhetoricians, famed for her learning, a sort of modern Oxford, Edinburgh or Boston, was notorious for vice and crime. Many of the brainiest congregations in cultured, hyper-refined New England have not spiritual power enough to withstand the most consumptive, the sallowest, the silliest, the puniest devil that hell ever turned out. Some of Boston's "four hundred" want nothiug better than the childish, effete religion of the heathen Burmese. Even though it is dubbed "Christian Science," that does not conceal its real character, for it is neither *Christian* nor *scientific.* We place no premium on ignorance. Thank God, we have a few scholarly, representative men who know the power of spirituality and who are sufficiently wise as to refrain from depending on their learning, eloquence or erudition, but put their confidence in the Holy Ghost himself. But, alas! many a poor preacher who is a D. D., LL. D., Ph. D., should add N. G.

Moreover, this power is not the power of wealth. It does not consist in flocks and herds, in broad acres of verdant land, in heaps of gold and silver, in stocks and bonds, nor in any form of material substance. The members of the Pentecostal Church had but little, and they sold what they did have and flung it cheerfully into the treasury of the Lord. In the world, congregations are often measured by their financial standing.

Not so above. God is not after money. He is no beggar. "The cattle on a thousand hills are his." In the hollow of his hand he holds the wealth of the universe. He hath need of nothing in the economic line.

In the early church money was a secondary matter, if it was a matter at all. To be poor did not disconcert the preachers of primitive days. "Silver and gold have I none," said Peter, as, in company with John, he met the cripple at the temple gate. In *these* days we hear of little else in the meetings of commit-mittees, boards of stewards, Ladies' Aid Societies, etc., but the threadbare cry of "Money! money! How shall we raise it?" "Where will we get the money?" is the first question when anything is to be undertaken in the church. Socials, entertainments, fairs, bazaars, festivals, broom-drills, kissing-parties, Mother Goose parties, poverty suppers, clam bakes, bean suppers, oyster stews (with few oysters), and every other devilish clap-trap that hell can invent are resorted to for the purpose of raising money to carry on God's holy work! What a shame that we are so poor that we must gull sinners out of their money by selling them ten cents worth of oysters for twenty-five cents! Our God is not a beggar.

When Christ commissioned his preachers, nothing was said about money except that a prohibition was made to the taking of much of it on their journeys. As the church has grown wealthy she has always lost her power to convict and convert sinners. Some monks were busily engaged in counting over huge piles of shining gold when Thomas Aquinas entered the room. "The time is no more when the church is compelled to say, 'Silver and gold have I none,'" remarked one of the counters. After a moment of grave thought the "Doctor Angelicus" replied, "True, and the time is no more when she can say, 'In the name of Jesus of Nazareth, rise up and walk.'" It is the general rule that the more expensive the church edifice, the less spirituality in the society; the higher the church steeple, the lower the real piety.

We make a great mistake in catering to moneyed men. The writer has often been surprised and pained to see a man in "poor raiment" come into the congregation, look in vain for a seat, and finally forced to be content with an inconvenient one by the door. But let the man in "fine raiment" and "gold ring" appear, and instantly a half-dozen people are on their feet motioning the visitor forward, pew-doors fly open as if by magic; all that the "moneyed man" may have a seat.

The strength of the church does not consist of brains, or numbers, or culture, or rhetoric, or schools. It does not reside in dignities, titles, sceptres, thrones, stocks or bonds. The strength of the ideal Pentecostal Church is the Holy Ghost himself. He and no other is the power of this great army of the Lord. He is not a mere influence; he is not the breath of God; he is not an emanation from Diety; he is not the abstract power of God. He is God himself, the third Person in the trinity. He comes into the church by coming into the individual members, and thus by his omnipotent energy he purifies, electrifies and endues her with power.

CHAPTER V.

A POWERFUL CHURCH—CONTINUED.

There is a widespread misapprehension as to what spiritual power really is. It is not power to found colleges nor maintain great universities. It is not power to teach the arts or sciences, to build pyramids, to drive steamships, to run express trains, or to establish telegraphic communication. These things are caused by other forces, other powers, than the purely Pentecostal. It is not power for political scheming or wise statesmanship. There are many things, good things, perhaps, which it is not the special function of this power to accomplish.

Positively, it is power to destroy the works of the devil and to save man from sin and from hell. But where, we ask, are the works of the devil? If they are to be destroyed, they must be located, and the power applied to them where they are. Some maintain that the works of the devil are located in the saloon, in the liquor traffic, and so we find men who give all their strength for the overthrow of *this* hellish business. Others believe that the brothel, social impurity and licentiousness are *the* works of the devil.

Laboring under this impression, certain persons bend all their energy to the work of the social purity movement. Still others assert that the works of the devil are housed in secret societies, and they therefore bend every energy toward the overthrow of these Christless institutions. We admit that the devil is actively engaged in the maintenance of these gigantic evils, and yet we must get on a warmer track than any of these if we are to find his work-shop, his place of business, where he turns out his samples. The place to which we have reference is the human heart. If from it the devil's works are cast out the man leaves the saloon and the woman forsakes the brothel; the lodge man renounces his order, and worldly entanglements are severed.

The works of the devil are not located in our heads, in our intellects. If they were, Yale, Harvard, Brown, Amherst, and Dartmouth might be able to cure the disease. Neither is sin to be located in the body. No medicine can reach it. Even if one be healed by Divine power he is not necessarily delivered from inbred sin. Many marvelous cases of Divine healing are recorded in which the healed person was not sanctified. Sin is located in the *heart*, the spiritual, affectional nature of man. "Out of the *heart*," says Christ, "proceed evil thoughts," etc.

The Pentecostal power, the power of the Holy

Ghost, lays an axe at the very root of the tree, and, instead of dealing with branches and limbs, it attacks and destroys all roots of pride, anger, jealousy, malice, envy, strife, impatience, worldliness, unholy ambition, lust, and all impurity even in its most complex ramifications. It delivers us from all grumbling, whining, peevishness, fretfulness, fearfulness, sensitiveness and touchiness. It blessedly relieves us of all pomp, gusto and brag. The bluster and braggadocio of swaggering depravity entirely departs. That yeasty "puff" so characteristic of carnality when lauded and commended has yielded to a more solid and satisfactory tissue. Men may flatter and use "soft soap," but the Holy Ghost man does not puff up; they may criticise and severely censure and mercilessly condemn, and yet he does not puff down.

This power of Pentecost delivers a man from thirst for place in the church. No one holds a position that he wants for himself. He is not offended if others are used more than he. He is not "hurt" if others are honored and he is slighted. He rejoices in the prosperity of another, and that not with a smirking, hypocritical semblance of rejoicing, but with a real, heartfelt gladness that "in honor the other" is preferred.

"The Holy Ghost coming upon" us furnishes such power that all work runs easily. "My yoke is easy," says the Lord. One who has received the gift of the Holy Ghost never has to rely on human dependencies or outward circumstances. The writer was one day sailing down the Narragansett Bay in company with a member of his church when suddenly the brother called his attention to the "Walker Armington," remarking that it was the only vessel of its kind on the Atlantic Coast. "What is there peculiar about this vessel?" he asked, for it was but one of the many beautiful four-masted schooners which filled the bay. "Notice," said the gentleman, "the black smoke issuing from the top of one of the masts. The schooner is fitted out with an engine, and thus is able to sail up and down this crooked channel without requiring the assistance of a tug." "That," I said to myself, "is but a symbol of my own experience. Since I received the Holy Ghost I am not dependent upon any fleet of tugs."

That queenly, graceful "floating palace," the "Connecticut," was approaching our Providence harbor one morning in a heavy fog. As the steamer rounded Field's Point the pilot failed to hear the fog-horn, and the huge ship slipped onto the bar. The full strength of the massive engines only lurched the steamer from side to side and ground her hull more firmly in the sand. Tugs were sent for; but the combined efforts of many tugs only showed their utter incompetency to float the vessel. What was to be done? There *was* but one thing to do. Wait until God's moon by the magic of its attraction had lifted the sea five feet, and then it was that the "Connecticut" floated with perfect ease. Five feet of God's water under the ship's keel were worth more than all the tugs. So with us when we cease our own struggles. When we stop trusting in our friends to tug us loose, when we turn our eyes from all things human up to the great God, then he will lift us with the tide of love that swells in his bosom and waft us to a calm haven with perfect ease. Instead of tearing us to pieces by pulling at us, he gently puts the "everlasting arms" beneath us and raises us and bears us swiftly away from all bars and shoals. It is so delightfully easy when we let *him* do it all. We are informed by false teachers that "God helps the man who helps himself," and that God will not do anything for us that we can do for ourselves. But this is not Bible. It is damaging teaching. Thus thousands seek God only to supplement their own unholy efforts. They call on him only when *they* have completely failed. In the *utmost extremity* God is to be resorted to. What a pity! All our doings are deadly. We reach a point where we must do nothing: Christ must do all. "Ye shall not fight in this battle." "The battle is not yours but God's." "It is not by might nor by power, but by my Spirit, saith the Lord." "For he that is entered into his rest he also hath ceased from his own works as God did from his." When we receive the Holy Ghost we retire from business; we are then at leisure; we enter upon a Sabbath of rest that never ends, a Sabbath that must not be broken.

So long as we endeavor to care for ourselves, God will give up to us the entire monopoly of the business, and it is awfully hard work. But when we receive him, he takes entire charge and manages everything. We go out of business. We sell the entire stock, the fixtures, the stand, everything to him. We make a clear warranty deed to all we have; we turn in all, past, present and future, things known and unknown, future friends and foes, wealth or poverty, prosperity or adversity, coming conquest and seeming failure. Our reputation is included in the consecration. No longer will we seek it, defend it, or try to take care of it. We will quit itching to run down every little rumor the devil sets flying from lip to lip concerning us. We transfer ourselves with all our belongings over to God. We surrender the papers, we hand over the keys. God cancels the mortgages, pays the taxes, and keeps up repairs on the property. What a relief! Hallelujah!

CHAPTER VI.

A WITNESSING CHURCH.

"Ye shall be witnesses unto me." "They all began to speak." Spontaneously, instinctively, the witnessing tongue began to vibrate. Never once did the fire-touched disciples think of sitting down and holding a silent meeting. Equally foreign to them was the idea of hiring some one to speak for them or to sing for them. Testimony is the invariable concomitant of *life* in a church. Only when the church has drifted from her great spiritual center and ignored and rejected the Holy Ghost has she lost her testimony.

Numerous and diverse are the substitutes offered in place of this God-ordained and God-originated way of stopping the mouth of the world and raining heart-thrilling conviction upon the soul. Sometimes increased religious activity is proffered in lieu of testimony. However good this activity may be, it will never produce the end God intended testimony should produce. If the "great unwashed," the unsaved and unattracted about us are ever reached it will not be by essays on the harmony between science and religion. It will not be by learned treatises in defense of orthodoxy, or rose-scented, high-school-girl themes on "The March of the Nineteenth Century." These subjects may be of value to the preacher for mental discipline, but they are not only hard on a congregation but they utterly fail to save men from sin and a yawning hell!

A live church has a ceaseless ringing testimony. It has been well said that "A voiceless church is a powerless church." The Holy Ghost is the power for witnessing. He gives the testimony irresistible, unanswerable force. Men are reached not by argument, not by logical syllogisms, but by the testimony of really *live witnesses*, witnesses who have convictions born of certainty, who "speak that they do know." An objector can meet logic with logic, Greek roots with Greek roots, and the jargon of the schools with the same language; but he does not know what to do with *experience*, with what is positively *known*.

The devil's hottest persecution has always been directed against public witnessing. No one has ever suffered opposition for having piety in the heart merely; a few have encountered it for possessing godliness in the home; but the concentrated powers of earth and hell have ever been marshalled against public witnessing for Jesus. Rome's energies were exhausted in an attempt to crush the testimonies of the early churches. Ten fierce persecutions followed one another in quick succession. To be a witness meant to die, so that the word for witness (martyr) came to mean one who died for "the testimony of Jesus." But although hundreds of thousands spilled their blood yet the churches "multiplied and grew."

During the severe persecution of the early Quakers, when the adult members were imprisoned until there were none to keep up the public meetings, and it seemed as if this public testimony must cease, the children of the Friends, ten, twelve and thirteen years of age, met together and maintained the meetings while the fathers and mothers were in jail. Persecution, fierce and savage, greeted this youthful piety, but no power on earth or in hell could withstand their fire-filled witnessing. Red-hot rings were put on their tongues, and yet with indistinct, pitiful words they would still testify.

On one occasion three Quaker ministers were to be burned at the stake. The persecutors so arranged that the second and third should witness the death of the first, while the third was to behold the torture of both first and second. The three men agreed among themselves that the one who was burned first should, if his faith failed not, testify in the last moment of his consciousness by lifting up one hand, thus encouraging the other two. The first of the martyrs was led forth, tied to the stake, and enveloped by the rising flame. When he had burned almost to a crisp and they thought he would never move again, the sufferer lifted both hands over his head and clapped them three times. Though racks and dungeons and stakes are no longer in vogue, yet testimony is as much needed and as much hated as in the days of virulent, violent persecution.

When spirituality runs low in the church, class-meetings, prayer-meetings, covenant-meetings and testimony-meetings are sparsely attended, while in the same church throngs crowd to the fairs, the festivals, the bazars, the bean suppers, the donkey parties and the entertainments. Contrast with this condition of affairs a church "filled with the Spirit." Witnessing meetings are large and the childish rattles which we have mentioned are no longer needed.

When a man really receives the Holy Ghost, he *wants* to testify to what God has done for and in him. An impelling power constrains him to speak even in the gaunt face of grim death. If those who have died for Jesus' sake had but held their peace there would have been no martyrs. They were offered their lives if they would but keep still. No one told them not to "live it" but "*teach* no more in this name." All the opposition which pitted itself against Jesus was due to his public preaching and work. If he had moved around quietly, if he had delivered lectures on the Talmud instead of preaching the "Sermon on the Mount," if he had talked hazily of evolution instead of exhorting to holiness, the Jews would never have risen to put him to death. "Live it, but keep still about it," says the devil; but life is made up largely of what we say, and he who shuts out the Son of God from his speech debars Him from his heart. Let him refrain from a confession of the Holy Ghost, and he will not have power to live it anywhere. "Heart-faith" and "lip-confession" are twins, and must not, can not, be separated.

CHAPTER VII.

KNOWS NO SEX.

The ideal Pentecostal Church is without distinction as to the prominence given to the sexes. The women were equally honored with the men when the Spirit was poured out. "These all continued with one accord in prayer and supplication *with the women.*" "I will pour out my Spirit upon all flesh, and your sons and your *daughters* shall prophesy." "And also upon the servants and upon the *handmaids* in those days will I pour out my Spirit." Women, as well as men, are to prophesy when this holy baptism with the Spirit shall be administered. No reference is made in Scripture to the ruling of a General Conference or an Ecumenical Council.

Originally, woman was not only man's helpmeet but his equal. "They twain shall be one flesh." Sin cursed and degraded her, until in dark heathendom we find her as man's slave. She is a beast of burden in many pagan countries. Enslaved, degraded, abused, she is brought lower than the brute. Well might Mr. Moody say, "I would rather be a donkey in heathen lands than a woman," for in those countries men set a greater value many times upon their donkeys than upon their wives.

But just in proportion as the grace of God and the light of the Gospel are shed abroad, in that proportion woman is elevated, until at Pentecost she stands, a second Eve, by the side of her husband, sharing in the beatific blessings of the baptism with the Spirit.

Taking humanity as a whole, it may be said with confidence that more genuine New Testament piety can be found among women than among men. From the days of Pentecost until this hour, whenever Holy Ghost revivals have been produced, holy women have mothered them, nursing into strength and vigor the nascent converts. Many an Elizabeth Frye, or Mary Fletcher, or Sibyl Jones has blessed the world with her holy ministry. The world will never get over the fragrant effects of the loving lives of these saints.

Nothing but jealousy, prejudice, bigotry, and a stingy love for bossing in men have prevented woman's public recognition by the church. No church that is acquainted with the Holy Ghost will object to the public ministry ot women. We know scores of women who can preach the Gospel with a clearness, a power, and an efficiency seldom equalled by men.

Sisters, let the Holy Ghost fill, call and anoint you to preach the glorious Gospel of our Lord.

CHAPTER VIII.

A LIBERAL CHURCH.

"And sold their possessions and goods, and parted them to all as every man had need." "Neither was there any among them that lacked, for as many as were possessors of lands or houses sold them and brought the price of the things that were sold and laid them down at the apostles' feet."

It is not the manner of liberality to which we desire to turn our attention, but to the spirit lying back of the generous action. The manifestation may alter, but the *spirit* of Pentecost never changes. From the days of the Apostles until this hour, whenever Pentecostal fire has fallen upon men or churches it has invariably burned the purse strings off and filled the possessor with the spirit of liberality. Spiritual lightning burns up all miserliness, stinginess, penuriousness, and covetousness, causing us to give in a princely way. We then for the first time, having our eyes illumined by the Holy Spirit, really perceive that "it is more blessed to give than to receive." We apprehend the law of Divine grace that the more we give the more we have.

This is, of course, contrary to all human law and precedent. It is diametrically opposite to human reasoning. The world says: "If you would be rich, save all you get and get all you can." God says: "Go sell all that thou hast and give to the poor." The world would have said that it was the sheerest folly to ask a widow woman who, with her son, was starving, to give away the last handful of meal in the barrel. But when she gave the precious food to God's prophet, God gave her a larder that never failed. It was God's way of opening up to the widow inexhaustible supplies. That handful of meal from the bottom of the barrel, doubtless stale and musty, was the key that unlocked the storehouse of boundless provisions.

"There is that scattereth and yet increaseth, and there is that withholdeth more than is meet but it tendeth to poverty." "The liberal soul shall be made fat, and he that watereth shall himself also be watered again." "He that soweth sparingly shall reap also sparingly: and he which soweth bountifully shall reap also bountifully." "Not grudgingly or of necessity, for God loveth a cheerful giver." "Honor the Lord with thy substance and with the firstfruits of all thine increase. So shall thy barns be filled with plenty and thy presses shall burst out with new wine." All that we give to the Lord is clear gain; all we save is lost. All we scatter will keep forever; all we keep will rot.

Our hoarded money will eat our flesh like fire. Many in our churches feel that every dollar they put into the Lord's work is just so much out of pocket. It is no wonder, when we remember this, that people cry, "Hard times" when money is needed. But the liberal giver never complains of hard times. A man who gives unstintedly and gives unto the Lord will always have something to give.

Those who complain of hard times in the churches which the writer has been permitted to serve have been those who give little or nothing. As a matter of fact, they *give* nothing, for they fail to pay even their rent, which is one-tenth of their income, to say nothing of a free-will offering over and above the just debt.

A Pentecostal Church will always have plenty of money without prostituting herself by unholy connection with this Godless, Christless world. She will never have to hire or sell herself to the world to get money. She will never become a slave to the Gentiles, feeding them with oysters, clams, cake, or ice cream. She will never need to turn the house of God into a second-rate theater, nor desecrate the temple with merchandise of any kind. Pentecostal liberality will liquidate our church debts, cancel our mortgages, and fill our church treasury to overflowing. It will send millions to the foreign field for the salvation of the heathen. When a man receives the Holy Ghost he ceases to put a five-dollar hat on his head and put five cents in the missionary collection; he will stop wearing a twenty-five-dollar overcoat until he can put more than a quarter in the basket for church purposes.

In one of our New England conventions a wealthy man and his wife came to the altar seeking the baptism with the Holy Ghost. They did not seem to be able to get the witness, and we wondered why. They were back again the next night. The usher informed us that, when the plates were passed, the gentleman put in one penny while his wife dropped in two. When the call was made, here came the couple again. We do not need to say that such stingy seeking as this was in vain. It is doubtful whether they received even three cents worth of spiritual blessing.

A Christian lady was complaining one day after she returned from church about the dullness of the sermon. Her little boy, who sat beside her in the pew, and had noticed the amount of her offering, spoke up quickly, "Why, mamma, what could you expect for a nickle!"

Nothing will ever protect the church from a bankrupt treasury and a burden of debt but this generosity-breeding flame from the skies. When it falls, pew-rents, entertainments, bazars, festivals, poverty suppers and all other devilish nonsense will disappear. Lord, send down this fire!

CHAPTER IX.

A DEMONSTRATIVE CHURCH.

"These men are filled with new wine." "It was noised abroad" and the people "were all amazed." The world admires and commends enthusiasm in everything but in religion. This country is a perfect hive of human industry. We hear the hum and roar and buzz of a million ceaseless activities. The very atmosphere is charged with commercial, political, social and intellectual enthusiasm. Indolence and sloth can hardly be tolerated. And yet with all this anything like healthy religious feeling is looked upon with suspicion, and the intoxication of the Spirit is branded as fanaticism. Thus thousands of people are silenced by adverse criticism.

Hundreds of churches are dying from propriety. We are not told specifically what the church at Pentecost did, but it is very evident that they conducted themselves in such a manner as to cause the public to think that they were all drunken. We also know that when Christians receive the Holy Spirit now, one will weep, another will shout, still another will jump, while a fourth will be still as death with a holy hush in his soul. But a spiritual church, from Pentecost to the present, has always been a noisy church. Pentecostal enduements are always "noised abroad." No one would suspicion the ordinary congregation of to-day as being intoxicated unless it should be thought that they were in the advanced stages, drowsiness for example.

Hosts of people have lost the light and joy from their souls simply because they have failed, refused or neglected to give expression to the movings of the Spirit within. Many have confessed that they have felt again and again that they ought to say "Amen!" or "Praise the Lord!" or "Hallelujah!" in the public congregation of the people, but they refrained and in a short time had nothing to say "Hallelujah!' about.

In the early days of Quakerism, ministers often preached to acres and acres of people in open fields and, at such times, often hundreds would fall and lie on the ground under the slaying power of the Holy Spirit. Primitive Methodism not only had roomy "Amen-corners" filled with ringing "Amens" but shouting was general throughout the congregation. When Jonathan Edwards in the Congregational Church at Northampton preached "Sinners in the Hands of an Angry God" men grasped the pillars of the house, the backs of the pews, seeing, as they firmly believed, their feet slipping over the brink into a bottomless hell! Sobbing, weeping and wailing went up as from the damned themselves. It was estimated that five hundred souls were converted as a result of that sermon. The writer himself has seen six hundred people seeking God at one time.

During a camp meeting held at Portsmouth, Rhode Island, at the close of a sermon by one of our fire-crowned Holiness evangelists, sixty-five persons fell on their faces in the straw, without even the conventionality of an "invitation." At another time at the same camp a saintly brother was preaching when the power so fell upon the people that before the sermon was finished they began to come forward and prostrate themselves at the altar. Strong men would start toward the front and fall before they could reach the altar. This was continued until forty-two souls were on their faces crying unto God. And yet no one had hinted at having an altar service.

In January, 1894, the Holy Ghost fell upon a congregation of staid, conservative Quakers in Western Indiana. No one was asked to come to an altar; no effort was made to create any demonstration. One sister arose, came to the altar, and began to weep. One person after another followed until the large altar was completely filled. Then convicted souls began to go down in the body of the congregation. Away back by the door people knelt in prayer. All in a few moments, holy fire had fallen from the upper skies, swept over that large audience, and leveled hearts to the ground. Many were praying vocally at the same time (a thing quite out of order in a Quaker meeting). Sobbing and laughing, shouting and weeping, waving handkerchiefs and shaking hands, were seen in all parts of the house.

We are not encouraging thunder out of an empty cloud. We would not be understood as commending the rattle of an empty wagon. But that freedom from excitement which is so complimented by the world, and which is so common in nearly all Protestant churches, will never bring a harvest of souls.

The inexhaustible fertility of the soil in the Delta of the Nile is owing to the annual overflow of the river. Many a preacher, orthodox, upright, respectable, a strong reasoner, and a delightful speaker, never does much good because he is so excessively proper that he never enjoys a freshet. This preacher may challenge the admiration of the community with his eloquence; the people may listen with enrapt attention; they may express freely their approbation; and yet no one is saved from sin, no heart turned back from hell. Polished, refined, rhetorical, yet this preacher is powerless to turn men to God. What does it mean? He needs a freshet to fill his soul from bank to brae.

We are as much commanded not to quench the Spirit as we are commanded not to steal. The Holy Ghost will not remain in our hearts unless he can reign without a rival. He must not be grieved, repressed, insulted, or even questioned as to the propriety of the course He takes with us.

CHAPTER X.

IS MAGNETIC, ATTRACTIVE.

"Multitudes came together." One of the greatest problems of the day which confronts Protestantism is, "How shall we reach the masses?" Great convocations are held and from large platforms the question is discussed again and again. Ways and means are devised, but nothing adequate is found. A New York millionaire says, "The masses shall be reached and I will give a million and a half dollars to accomplish it." But money fails. Some one suggests that we get the most brilliant, eloquent, "drawing" ministers. But, alas, the preacher finds it hard work to draw sinners into the church over the obstructing corpses of dead church members. One suggests a new pipe organ, but as soon as the novelty of the great instrument wears off, the masses fail to come. A zealous æstheticist insists on more frescoing, a little more stucco work, a new carpet, and another canary in the choir. A gourmandizer suggests the possibility of drawing men by way of their stomachs. So the H. O. G. Society fits up a kitchen in the church and proceeds to sell thin oyster-soup at three hundred per cent. profit. But with all this nonsense of the church puttering around in a kitchen, the unsaved masses are unreached and unattracted. The Committee on "Ways and Means" finally says, "We must have a new church." So one hundred and fifty thousand dollars worth of stone and brick and mortar is piled up and surmounted by a weather-vane, emblematic of the wind-influenced congregation worshipping beneath. This mass of matter is dubbed "a church." But, alas, while its superb auditorium will seat twelve hundred easily, the Reverend Mr. Jones, D.D., LL.D., Ph.D., reads his infantile sermonette on Sunday morning to an audience of three hundred and fifty!

We meet in minister's meetings to discuss and deplore the situation. We listen to long essays on the subject in which everything is suggested as remedial except the one, and only one, thing that will prove efficacious. Who dares to say that the ministers themselves should tear down their lightning-rods, go down on their faces in an "upper room," and tarry until the heavenly flame leaps the chasm from celestial altar to human heart, consuming ministerial and church pride, delivering the ministry from false dignity, hell-concocted starch, and bringing it on a level with the people it was designed to help? Then we would depend on God, instead of on a few brains. We would rely on the Holy Ghost rather than on "big sermons," spread-eagle rhetoric, and highfalutin bombast. The blessed Spirit would then accomplish what our efforts, our movements and our methods can never acoomplish. This spiritual electricity from high heaven will burn up our rubbish, attract the attention of the world, and bring back to the church the "lost art" of soul-saving.

When Moses was traveling along the highway at Horeb he saw a bush on fire, and yet it was not consumed. "And Moses said I will now turn aside and see this great sight why the bush is not burnt." Everyone admits that this is a hurrying, busy time. It is a fast age. "Life is too short," men can not wait. Swifter than the turning of this eastward-wheeling earth is man's means for the transference of thought, so that Boston news is read in San Francisco two hours before its *dated* occurrence. But with all the competition and push and bustle of this rapid life of ours, if a church should get on fire with holy flame the people *en masse* would turn aside to see "this great sight."

Note the agility and celerity with which people turn out to a fire. The writer was stopping in an eastern city when at midnight the fire-bell began to ring. He threw up the window and saw people from every direction pouring forward towards the building from whose roof the flames were rising. All classes and conditions were mingled in the excited, interested throng He saw among others an old white-haired man on crutches hobbling along toward the scene of the conflagration. The lame and the lazy, the rich and the poor, the high and the low, the white and the black, all are fascinated by a fire. A fire in the pulpit and a fire in the pew will draw the multitudes together. God's description, his pen-picture, of a minister is "a flame of fire." This pulpit-flame six feet long and white-hot will attract all classes within its sweeping range.

The Pentecostal Church spent no money in advertising. She had in her attractions of the most magnetic character. Sensationalism will fail, as it always has. The artful skill of man will not succeed. The writer is acquainted with a church in a New England city where for thirty months this holy fire attracted the crowds, summer and winter, week in and week out. During the hot months of July and August, when the greater part of other churches were gone to the sea-shore to keep cool (as if a refrigerator needed cooling), this Pentecostal Church was packed to the door while people were turned away for want of standing-room. A fire-crowned church will never want for crowds.

CHAPTER XI.

PUTS PEOPLE UNDER CONVICTION.

"They were pricked in their hearts." "And when he is come he will reprove the world of sin and of righteousness and of judgment." The blessed Holy Ghost "when he is come" into the hearts of believers will convict sinners of sin. He is invariable in the faithfulness with which he answers the faith of Christians in this matter.

The conviction that fell upon the people in Bible times is comparatively rare in these days. Genuine Scriptural conversions, however, are preceded by deep and pungent conviction for sin. Jesus came to save, not the righteous, but the sinner conscious of his sinfulness. He seeks the lost; and unless men find out that they are lost, they will never be saved. We make a sad mistake when we receive persons into church membership who do not give evidence of being saved. The popular revivals of the last quarter of a century have been very superficial. The method which consists of raising the hand, signing a card, entering an enquiry room—where the "seeker" (?) sits bolt upright like a post and coolly converses on the subject of religion—and finally "taking it by faith," is an awful fraud and a burlesque on the true revival. It is a deception that is appalling. Thousands are swept into the "church" and from thence into hell! Souls are dropping into the mouth of the pit in platoons and battalions for the want of men who preach a faithful gospel. The superficial revivals to which we have referred only make it more difficult for those who do thorough work.

Even among some so-called Holiness teachers and workers there is a tendency to superficiality. Many seekers are taught to make the profession the condition of obtaining the grace. "Just claim it by faith and *say*, 'It is done,' and it *is* done." You ask these wrongly-instructed people if they know they are saved or sanctified. The answer is: "Well, I have just taken Christ for my Saviour, or Sanctifier," as the case may be. "I am simply trusting. I have not had the witness of the Spirit, but I do not depend on feeling. I am just standing on the promise." This whole thing is nonsense and a farce. In the first place, the essence of a promise is contained in its fulfillment. It is folly to talk about standing on a promise if the promise is not fulfilled. Faith is not an effort. Faith rests and *always* gets an answer. Faith springs up readily in thoroughly submitted soil. Not one person in a thousand has any real difficulty with his *faith* in getting divine experiences. If pardon is the thing sought, repentance is usually the catch. If the seeker is after a clean heart the shortage is in his consecration.

When a sinner has done a thorough job of repenting, the grace of faith is present to cause faith to spring up. When a believer has gone down, down to the very bottom in his consecration until he has lost confidence in himself and in everybody and everything else to sanctify him, it will be the easy, yea, the natural thing for him to do to fall over on God and trust Him. Some say, "I have taken it by faith, but I have not received the evidence." Impossible. Faith itself "is the evidence of things not seen," and real faith always brings the witness of the Spirit. The witness of the Spirit moves us out of the realm of faith into the province of knowledge. What we believed we have come to know. True faith is the *channel* through which we get all our blessings from God.

He who believes will hear from God. To claim that the conditions are all met and yet no news has been received from heaven is to give God the lie. Thus a "life of faith" is not a bread-and-water diet. It is a life in which we "eat bread without scarceness." We have three full meals a day if we want them. The man who "lives by faith" is much more likely to get porterhouse steak than chuck.

Superficiality must be avoided. The conviction of the Holy Ghost must be operative if men are to cry out, "Men and brethren, what shall we do to be saved?" He is the "Executive of the Godhead," and He alone is competent to guide souls. We make a mistake in most of our altar services by talking so much to seekers. No one can talk them through, or sing them through, or shout them through. If *you* do the work you will have to do it again in a short time. The Holy Spirit can convict souls until they will be glad of a chance to rush to the altar and cry out to God. If we tease people to an altar and tease them to pray and tease them to believe and tease them to testify, we will have the endless task of teasing on our hands, and even then we can't keep them from backsliding. But if, on the other hand, souls are sufficiently convicted to break up and cry out and pray through to complete victory, they will not need any one to tell them that they are saved; they will know it.

One of the great mistakes of this age is that many think and say that "Splendid ends can be reached only by the use of splendid means." The demand, therefore, is for splendid means. But this premise is not true. God can do great things with a "Moses' rod," a "ram's horn," a "shepherd's sling," or an "ox-goad." He can take the things that are not and bring to naught the things that are. A strand of copper wire is dead and powerless of itself. You may insert it in a keg of gunpowder without any startling results It is perfectly harmless. But let the electric current be turned on to this ineffectual wire, and thousands of tons of rock are hurled into the air. Let the submarine cable receive the wondrous spark, and under thousands of miles of unfathomed sea it flashes the message of God.

A common mistake among workers is to bow down to the implements used. God lets us catch a few fish, and we burn incense to our nets. We fail to give *him* the glory. May not God trust us with great success without danger of our filching the glory?

CHAPTER XII.

HAS HEALTHY CONVERTS.

They are described as "continuing steadfast in the apostles' doctrine and fellowship." A healthy mother gives birth to healthy children, and a church spiritually strong will have strong and vigorous converts. It is of incalculable value to have a good start in anything. This is eminently true in religious experience. There is such a thing as being well-born spiritually. A feeble church, if she have converts at all, will have feeble ones. She may have life and power enough to put sinners under conviction and, perhaps, get them to a place of prayer, but she will fail in faith and prayer to bring them forth, to get them to a place of victory.

A revival which does not greatly increase and strengthen the spiritual vigor of the church is superficial. Much of the so-called revival work is so shallow that the thousands of counted "converts" can not be located in four months after the special services have closed. They can not be found in the prayer-meeting. They are absent from the class-meeting. They do not attend the Sunday preaching services. The only evidence of their religious existence is the name on the church register. A union meeting of one hundred days was held in one of our large cities, under the leadership of a noted evangelist. Hundreds of persons signed cards and made profession of religion. In a few months the converts were not to be seen. Indeed, the pastors themselves confessed that their churches were in a worse condition than before the special services. Another evangelist went to a certain city and began preaching an old-fashioned, fiery gospel. His "pulpit manners" were uncouth and objectionable. The truth itself was sent forth in great rugged chunks, with edges and corners almost incapable of polish. Even the pastor was disturbed. But the evangelist continued in the fear of God, and the Lord vindicated His truth, sending power and conviction on the people until three hundred and twenty-five souls made profession of salvation, joining the church on probation. At the end of six months two hundred and seventy-five of this number were received into full membership.

We read of strong converts at Thessalonica. Paul says of them, "Our gospel came not unto you in word only but also in power," and they "received the word in much affliction with joy in the Holy Ghost." They were such strong converts that though they had not been sanctified wholly yet they were "ensamples to all that believe" and their "faith Godward" was "spread abroad." What was the secret of this vigor? Paul, himself a man filled with the Holy Ghost, began his ministry among them by "reasoning with them, opening and alleging *out of the Scriptures.*" He had no stock of thrilling anecdotes; no heart-rending deathbed scenes to stir up the people. He preached a gospel that carried with it conviction for sin. It so stirred the conscience and so effectively set in array the sins of the sinner before his eyes that souls were eager to call on God for pardon. It was not Paul's "personal magnetism" or eloquence that produced these results. He declared that he preached through "infirmity of the flesh." "I was with you," he says, "in weakness and in fear and in much trembling and my speech was not with enticing words of man's wisdom but in the demonstration of the Spirit and of power that your faith should not stand in the wisdom of men but in the power of God." Paul denies that he is strong either in natural or acquired ability. He is careful to say that he preached "in the demonstration of the Spirit and of power" and for this very reason his converts "stood in the power of God."

If the Pentecostal Church had such a thing as a "minister's meeting" those who took part certainly did not meet to simply deplore the situation, read papers and pronounce the benediction. Decline in piety was felt to be a grave question. It was too serious a matter to be dealt with lightly. The backslidden brother must be restored by those "that are strong." Effective and divinely ordained methods must be used. We can hardly imagine a member of the early church suggesting church-work as a *remedy* or *preventative* for backsliding. It was not thought that the converts must have mission-work, a Sunday-school class, or a place in the choir to hold them in the church. More probably the converts did not feel that they needed to be held. Doubtless the question with them was "To whom shall we go?" for, on the day of Pentecost, they "that *gladly* received the word were baptized." Too many of the so-called "converts" of to-day are coaxed and almost compelled to join the church. No wonder that they have so little heart for real church-work and very quickly drift by the law of gravitation and consciousness of kind to their own company.

To be well-born spiritually means that the convert have a clear, satisfactory witness of the Spirit with his own that he is born of God. After this preliminary work of grace is completed in the heart, if he is instructed and encouraged to "tarry until" he is "endued with power from on high," he will continue steadfastly in the apostles' faith, doctrine and fellowship. The baptism with the Holy Ghost is the only safeguard against backsliding. Some one has said that "God justifies us that he may sanctify us, and he sanctifies us that he may keep us justified." There are few people living justified lives who are not also living sanctified lives. We hear a great deal said about "sinning and repenting" among Christian people, so-called. That there is much sinning among those who talk in this way, we doubt not; but that there is much hearty repentance, we can not believe. Repentance of sin means forsaking sin with no secret purpose of remaining a sinner. This attitude of the soul God demands before he pardons. God certainly has no more tolerance for sin in the heart or life of a Christian than he has in a sinner. One would suppose that if leniency were granted anywhere it would be in the case of those who do not know by experience what it means to have sins pardoned. But God hates sin wherever found, and gives no license in any instance for its committal or retention. We therefore believe the number of those who thus forsake sin and repent of it every day to be very small. They either give up in despair or seek and obtain a grace which keeps them *from* sin.

"They continued steadfastly" in prayer. The Pentecostal Church was not divided into praying and non-praying members. All of the members were praying people, and prayer became such a fixed habit with them that they were steadfast in it. There were offered no inducements to attend prayer-meeting, such as cake, coffee, and a "short, spicy service." Ah, nc; they made no stipulations as to the length of their prayers. The lone Man on the mountain deep in midnight prayer was ever before them. The Holy Ghost taught the early saints what to pray for, and they received answers. They "stirred up themselves to take hold on God." They knew how to continue in prayer and "watch in the same." Baxter stained his study walls with praying breath. Epaphras, one of the members of the early church, "always labored abundantly in prayers." All members of the Pentecostal Church do the same. If our fathers had known as little of the power of prayer as many church members dc to-day, some of our great religious bodies would never have existed. If they had indulged in the practice of resorting to everything else before calling on God, as is sc common now, we would have had no great denominations.

Someone asked an old saint what she thought of the new minister, who had just delighted the body of his hearers with an eloquent sermon. "I do not know," she answered, "I have not heard him pray." The Pentecostal Church took everything to God. He must redress all their wrongs, defend their characters, and protect their property. "Be careful for nothing, but in everything by prayer . . . let your requests be made kncwn unto God,'' was the exhortation ever ringing in their ears They lived in an atmosphere of prayer, and died praying, "Lord Jesus, receive my spirit.''

There is a great demand in these days for a race of moral heroes and heroines—men and women who can withstand the surging tide of worldliness and the spirit of compromise, and who can not be bribed, bought, or brow-beaten into the desertion of the truth.

If the Holy Ghost was allowed to convict people for sin, and they were taught to look to God for the witness of their salvation, instead of relying on themselves, their feelings, the word of the evangelist, or the opinion of the pastor, God would answer them from heaven and they would desire no further evidence. They would then remain "steadfast, unmovable, always abounding in the work of the Lord.'' Amen.

CHAPTER XIII.

A JOYFUL CHURCH.

The ideal Pentecostal Church is a joyful church. "Did eat their meat with *gladness* and singleness of heart." "And the disciples were filled with *joy* and with the Holy Ghost."

One of the legitimate and normal products of Pentecost is joy. "In His presence there is fullness of joy." "These things have I spoken unto you that my joy might remain in you, and that your joy might be full." It must have astonished the sorrowing disciples to hear the "Man of Sorrows," on his way to a bloody scourging, to a crown of thorns, and to a cruel cross, talking about joy, fullness of joy, joy enough to give to all his grief-stricken disciples.

We are distinctly told that "the joy of the Lord is our strength." A sad Christian is always a weak Christian. God never sends a discouraged person to help some one else who is discouraged. We can not impart to others that which we do not ourselves possess. Samuel Rutherford, in one of his delightful letters, says: "A river of God's unseen joy hath flowed from bank to brae over my soul since I parted with you." One great difference between salvation and religion is with regard to this element of joyfulness. Religion is often gloomy and long-faced; salvation is bright, happy, cheerful, sparkling and joyful. The countenances of the heathen are gloomy. They are invariably religionists. Similarly in civilized countries thousands upon thousands of religionists look down their noses, extend their faces, and are profoundly sad. But God is not down, but up. He "went *up* from talking with Abraham." Jesus "went *up*" from Mt. Olivet. If we would find God, if we would see Jesus, our gaze must be an *upward* gaze.

The countenance of a fire-baptized Christian is one of radiance, gladness and sunshine. A reporter said, in describing one of our great camp meetings: "One thing which characterized all faces was joyfulness."

Moreover, the joy of Pentecost is permanent, uninterrupted. There are depths in the ocean that are unaffected by tempest and storm. Quietude eternal prevails. So there may be a joy in the soul so deep, so abiding, that no outward circumstance or event or perplexity can disturb or dismay.

Pentecostal joy is often uncontainable, unmanageable, irrepressible. Its possession often causes the possessor to be grievously misunderstood, for he laughs when others would weep, he sings when others would sigh, he shouts when others would sulk and pout, he dances when the heavens are black with disappointment. When his heart and life are filled with unutterable sorrow, he smiles even through his tears. He is never offended. Indeed it is sometimes said of him that he does not know enough to know when he is insulted. This latter is certainly a blissful ignorance.

Jesus was anointed with the oil of gladness above his fellows, and he is the leader of that happy band who shall "come to Zion with songs and everlasting joy upon their heads," who "shall obtain joy and gladness, and sorrow and sighing shall flee away." At creation's dawn "the morning stars sang together," and until sin came and marred all, joy and gladness were everywhere. Jesus redeems us, the Holy Ghost restores to us our lost joy, so that we never think of combining salvation and melancholy.

Even the Jews, under the earlier dispensation, had spells of rejoicing, which is more than many professed Christians have to-day. God's people in those times had three or four great religious (in the better sense) picnics each year, and at the closing festival of the year the whole nation went into booths for an entire week of rejoicing. At one of these feasts Nehemiah read the law and called upon the people to rejoice that the desolation of Zion was removed. But they, like many to-day, thought they must celebrate with *tears.* Nehemiah insisted that it was no time for mourning.

It was a holy day, and holiness and sorrow do not go well together. Tears should be a thing of the past. Let us have that strength which springs from the joy of the Lord.

How much more one can do when the heart is joyful and free from care. The writer was once pastor for four years in a mining district. He has often been struck with the whistling and humming of tunes by the miners as they started down into the damp, dark mines. Thank God, we can whistle even in the blackest and darkest places in life's pathway.

Did you ever stand and watch the sailors as they heave their great loads into the hold of the vessel? They are going on a voyage and they sing, and in their singing the great bales are tumbled about like feathers.

See the soldier trudging a dreary march across an arid plain! See him working in the trenches! Suddenly he hears the beat of the drum, the shrill cry of the fife, and the chorus of the battle song, and his heart swells, and he is stronger.

A fireman is vainly attempting to reach an upper window where a wee child is gasping for breath. He is almost despairing. Some one in the crowd says, "Cheer him!" and from a thousand throats goes up a shout of encouragement, and the arm strengthens, the head clears and the man dashes through the smoke and flame and rescues a life.

There are great corporations and business enterprises in this country which will not employ a man if he is known to be unhappy in his domestic relationships. His services are worth more if he is happy in his home. Now, if joy is so valuable in secular things, how much more in spiritual! God wants a happy people, for no other kind can fairly represent him.

O brother, are you training in that procession, who, loaded with spices, are on their way to the tomb to embalm the body of Jesus? Have you never heard of the resurrection? He is not here. He is risen. Go into Galilee and tell the disciples. Turn your back on the grave and with sunshine and gladness speak of his triumph. Most of professed Christians show by their faces that they are headed toward the graveyard, and many of them are as cold and stiff as the tombstones themselves.

Pentecost will give us joy in persecution. "They took joyfully the spoiling of their goods." "They counted it all joy that they were counted worthy to suffer shame for his name." Bunyan wrote his immortal "Pilgrim's Progress" in the old Bedford jail. He says, "So I was led home to prison. And I sat me down and wrote and wrote, because joy did make me write." That old, damp, dingy dungeon, ill-lighted and poorly supplied with even necessities, was heaven on earth to the saintly spirit.

It was this joy that Paul and Silas had at midnight when they sung themselves out of prison at Philippi. It was this joy that caused the triumphant songs of the martyrs to ring out so clearly through the passages and cells of gaols, transforming the miserable dungeons into golden palaces. The shining luster of Stephen, the angel-faced, was seen even amidst the showers of stones, because he possessed this joy. To no other source can we trace the radiance which overspread the countenance of Mary Dyer, at the place of execution on Boston Common. For hours after her seraphic spirit had winged its flight, the light still played in her face.

This joy of which we write is worth more to the Church than millions of money. Some people's presence is a very benediction to your home, and when they go you feel that they leave a fragrance and a savor of blessedness that will benefit you forever.

When Israel was thirsty at Beer, Moses had the people gather together while the princes digged in the sand. But there was no water until Israel sang this song, "Spring up, O well." *Then* God gave water. It means something to have faith and joy enough to sing over an empty hole in the ground, to sing when there is nothing apparently to sing about. But *this* is just where faith operates, *when there is nothing in sight*.

Pentecost will give us joy in the night, cause us to sing in the blackest storm. Glory! Hallelujah! Amen and amen!

CHAPTER XIV.

THE PENTECOSTAL CHURCH A UNIT.

"They were all with one accord in one place." "Continuing daily with one accord in the temple." Pentecost provides for the only true basis of unity. The baptism with the Holy Ghost is the only experience that will ever bring about the fulfillment of that prayer of Jesus in the seventeenth chapter of John's Gospel, the twenty-third verse, "That they all may be one."

Education, legislation, organization and coercion, one and all, utterly fail in making people of one heart. There is a vigorous attempt being made to preserve unity in organizations by legislating out of the church all who do not agree with the predominant party. But this is a great failure. Nothing can be *stamped out*, not even error. The more a church legislates against so-called or real heretics, the more heresy will be stirred up. There is more or less heterodoxy in every one of us until it is burned out by the furnace of the "upper room." If education succeeds in uniting men's heads, even then it utterly fails to unify their hearts; only the Holy Ghost can do that. The writer was brought up a Quaker after the strictest sect of our religion, but since Pentecost he finds himself in the sweetest fellowship with Spirit-baptized Christians of all denominations. We have sat on our great camp-meeting and convention platforms, working together with men and women of God for ten days without ever thinking to ask of what sect they were members.

We have again and again known church committees to go long distances in order to effect the restoration to unity of people engaged in a church brawl. Discordant elements were brought together, some concessions were made on all sides, and the committee returned much gratified. But lo! before the members of this committee had reached their homes the trouble was worse than before. The only cure for discord is fire.

Pentecost brings us into touch with the best people of all ages. By this baptism we are brought into the closest relationship. Brother Updegraff said: "I have noticed that men who are great on Quakerism, or great on Methodism, are usually light on salvation." Is it not true that the larger views we get of Christ the smaller grows our denominationalism? Some maintain that they are free from sectarianism, and yet seek to justify themselves in denominationalism. This is ordinarily a distinction without a difference.

If unity is ever to be effected and maintained, if

orthodoxy is to be conserved, it must all be brought about by Pentecost. There is more real unity between a Salvation Army soldier and a Spirit-filled High Church Episcopalian, than can be found between any two theologians bound together simply by their creed. Oh, that this burning flame might be permitted to come upon the Church, both pulpit and pew! If the men who occupy our college chairs and who fill our stately pulpits, could only experience this sin-consuming holocaust, it would free us of this excess of human smartness, theories of evolution, higher criticism and skepticism. The rubbish would disappear; soul-saving would again be common and great and permanent revivals would break out in our centers of learning. It was not syllogisms nor arguments which convinced the great convocation on Mount Carmel. It was fire, vaulting over the walls of God's heaven, that turned back the rising tide of infidelity and established the authority of the one true God. When Pentecost is come again we will be of one accord, and all will say, "The Lord He is God! The Lord He is God!"

CHAPTER XV.

DIVINE HEALING.

The tendency of this age is to eliminate from Christianity all that is miraculous. Man is exalted and God is relegated to the past. A most vigorous effort is made to explain all that appears supernatural in the Bible on rational and materialistic grounds. Human smartness has reduced the system of nature to a self-acting automatic mechanism.

To many Christianity is only a system of theology and ethics. We are told by those who ought to know better that the miracles of Christ were simply a sort of divine credential for the purpose of proving his divinity and rightful authority, and that as soon as that was accomplished they ceased, as being no longer necessary. If Christianity needed credentials when the Son of God himself walked through this land with all power in heaven and in earth, certainly the weak, feeble, halting, hesitating, compromising Church of to-day needs something to establish its divinity before the people of this critical, analytical age. If the Christ needed credentials in Jerusalem, would not we need them in the jungles of Africa, in infidel France, or in

Unitarian New England? We confess to a feeling of need of something supernatural right here in the second city of New England.

Men who assert that miracles ceased with the Apostolic age only disclose their ignorance. All students of history know that the miraculous healing of the sick was common until the close of the first century, frequent throughout the second century, and occasional all through the third and fourth centuries, while signs and miracles have reappeared with every Holy Ghost revival since the Dark Ages.

George Fox relates many most remarkable instances of healing in the course of his ministry. John Wesley not only witnessed many instances of the healing of Christian men and women, but he even prayed for his horse, and it was healed! And yet many who claim to be followers of these men deny the power of God in this matter. It is not a little strange that many professed holiness people manifest extreme nervousness under a testimony to divine healing. But genuine holiness is responsible for the modern revival of healing, for nothing but a Holy Ghost ministry will reproduce that stout faith in God which makes his power to heal operative. Shall we contend for the doctrine and experience of holiness and deny or even discount the legitimate outgrowth of the faithful spiritual preaching of that doctrine?

From God's word there can be no appeal. If God makes any truth prominent in his Word we can not afford to neglect or ignore it, much less oppose it, because our experience has not measured up to it.

Let us stand for a few moments with uncovered heads and reverent, loving, obedient hearts while the oracles of God speak: "When the even was come they brought unto him many that were possessed of devils, and he cast out the spirits with his word and healed all that were sick: That it might be fulfilled which was spoken by Esaias, the prophet, saying, 'Himself took our infirmities and bare our sicknesses'" (Matt. viii. 16, 17).

"And Jesus went about all the cities and villages teaching in their synagogues and preaching the Gospel of the kingdom and healing every sickness and every disease among the people" (Matt. ix. 35).

"And Jesus went forth and saw a great multitude and was moved with compassion toward them, and he healed their sick" (Matt. xiv. 14).

"They sent out into all the country round about and brought unto him all that were diseased, and besought him that they might only touch the hem of his garment, and as many as touched him were made perfectly whole" (Matt. xiv. 36). "And great multitudes came unto him having with them those that were lame, blind, dumb, maimed, and many others, and cast them down at Jesus' feet and he healed them" (Matt. xv. 30). "And great multitudes followed him and he healed them there" (Matt. xix. 2).

"And the blind and the lame came to him in the temple and he healed them" (Matt. xxi. 14). "And he ordained twelve that they should be with him and that he might send them forth to preach and to have power to heal sicknesses and to cast out devils" (Mark iii. 14, 15). "And they cast out many devils and anointed with oil many that were sick and healed them" (Mark vi. 13). "Now when the sun was setting all they that had any sick with divers diseases brought them unto him and he laid his hands on every one of them and healed them" (Luke iv. 40). "Then he called his twelve disciples together and gave them power and authority over all devils and to cure diseases. And he sent them to preach the kingdom of God and to heal the sick" (Luke ix. 1, 2). "And they departed and went through the towns preaching the gospel and healing everywhere." "Is any sick among you? let him call for the elders of the church; and let them pray over him, anointing him with oil in the name of the Lord: and the prayer of faith shall save the sick and the Lord shall raise him up" (James v. 14, 15).

Now, that some have gone to unwarrantable extremes, and even into fanaticism, on divine healing, there can be no doubt. But may this not be said, as well, of experiences vastly more important? There is probably not a man in all our prisons who was placed there for counterfeiting the copper cent. So the devil counterfeits only good, God-sent and God-ordained things, and the more valuable the genuine the more elaborate and labored his imitation. Let us not reject the gold because there is some brass in circulation.

When Pentecost was come "the power of the Lord was present to heal." Let us then help each other's faith. It is much more Christ-like than to break off the heads of the tender shoots of trust in God and his power and willingness to heal.

Christianity is not an automatic, self-regulatory mechanism. It is supernatural, just as much so as in the days of the Apostles, and it has every moment the divine presence and living touch of its Author.

CHAPTER XVI.

A MISSIONARY CHURCH.

"And ye shall be witnesses unto me both in Jerusalem, and in all Judea, and in Samaria, and unto the uttermost part of the earth" (Acts i. 8).

Pentecost was the greatest missionary convention ever held, up to that time. From that gathering went out streams of holy fire in every direction, until they reached all of the then known world.

Jesus is a royal King with sovereign power and authority. As Jesus was appointed to administer in heaven and earth he, with perfect right, has appointed us to administer on earth. Invested with this authority he bids his disciples to go forth and establish his kingdom. The universality of our commission is sublime. But if the great and glorious work of evangelizing the world is to be completed, the Church must get an experience that will write on her heart in letters of fire the bare, hard facts of the world's destitution and fearful degradation. She must be oppressed with a heart-burden and a burning passion for souls. Nothing but Pentecost will ever place her beyond this cloud of rose-colored idealism about "the march of the nineteenth century" and belief that "the world is growing better and better." Until we are more deeply impressed with rugged facts than by a sickish sentimentality, nothing can be expected. And it is a bald fact that, with all our missionary effort, the world's population is advancing more swiftly than the Church is making converts. What if there *are* nearly eight hundred missionaries in China, there are three hundred and fifty million souls in that country who ought to have the Gospel. This, you see, is about four hundred and forty thousand to each missionary. There are six hundred and seventy-five missionaries in India, but there are more than three hundred million souls to be reached. Siam has ten million people, more than half a million to every male missionary. Ninety million people in the Soudan without the Gospel! Forty million in the Congo Free State have not heard of Christ. The continent of Africa has in all not less than two hundred million who never saw a Bible. There are in the world to-day eight hundred million souls who never heard the story of Bethlehem of Judea. All this is not because it is impossible for the Church to give these myriads of darkened souls the light, but because she has not had her Pentecost.

In these last days the Holy Spirit has breathed on human genius until time and space have been almost annihilated by the inventions of man. A modern man does as much in five years as an ancient did in fifty. A young girl goes around the world in seventy-five days. So great are facilities for travel that it is not only a possible thing, but a practicable, for a sanctified church to carry the Gospel to every creature beneath the skies in a single decade. But the self-seeking, ease-loving, heathen-forgetting, Christ-neglecting spirit of the Church will make such a blessed state of things impossible, without jagged bolts of Pentecostal lightning from God's heaven strike in the midst of the Church and transform her into the likeness of her Bridegroom.

Pentecostal experiences will fill our missionary treasuries, fire-crown our outgoing missionaries, and secure phenomenal results on the rocky fields of heathendom.

Of the eight thousand missionaries in the heathen world three-fourths of these are engaged in the work of education rather than of salvation. Jesus has never commanded the Church to educate, but to *preach the Gospel*, God's salvation. Teaching the heathen the arts, instructing them in agriculture, cooking, house-keeping, etc., is no doubt very praiseworthy work, but it must be remembered that none of these things are preaching the Gospel.

We repeat, if the Church would prepare herself by consecration and faith in God and the Pentecostal fire should fall, the whole heathen world would feel the shock as of a thousand earthquakes, and millions would be saved. Pentecost makes missionaries of all of us either at home or abroad, for one of the legitimate effects of real spirituality is an ardent desire to lead hearts to Jesus.

CHAPTER XVII.

OUT OF BONDAGE.

"And when I see the blood I will pass over you" (Ex. xii. 13). It is never wise to attempt to found a doctrine on a mere type or shadow or illustration. But when we find a truth well-founded in plain statement and clearly set forth in specific language in the Scriptures, also impressed and enforced by the Holy Ghost, we are justified in the careful study of the symbolic.

If you will open your Bible to the tenth chapter of I. Corinthians, and the 2d, 3d and 4th verses, you will find divine authority for saying that the exit of the children of Israel from Egyptian bondage is a type of the sinner's deliverance from the thraldom of sin and Satan. Egypt stands for the world, and Pharaoh is a striking symbol of the devil.

When Moses demanded Israel's release from bondage Pharaoh stoutly refused. But when forced by the judgments of God to yield a point, his first proposition was that they should "sacrifice in the land." He practically said: "I have no objection to your being religious and worshiping your God, only do not break away from us, do not forsake us." When a sinner is under conviction and is seriously contemplating getting free from sin and the world, Satan says: "Well, now, if you are going to be religious, that is all well enough, but do not forsake the world." The devil will even encourage the awakened soul to join a respectable church, for he himself is often very religious, and one of the most regular attenders of church, for in a large number of them he is a charter member. "It will make you peculiar to break with the customs, fashions and pleasures of the world," he says. Thus he is able, through the dearth and want of faithful, God-fearing preachers of the Gospel, to lead thousands to join the church without ever knowing what it is to be Scripturally converted. What a *fearful* time these ease-loving, pleasure-seeking, money-desiring and praise-hankering preachers and churches will have at the judgment! Hell is being peopled for the lack of a radical, aggressive, uncompromising Gospel, preached by daring ministers, who are not afraid to stand out against the rising tides of worldliness and selfishness.

When Moses said, "We will go three days' journey into the wilderness," Pharaoh replied, "I will let you go, only ye shall not go very far away." He doubtless thought that if they did not go so very far off, they would soon return. Thus it is when Satan can not prevent a sinner making *some* start, he seeks to make the start as insignificant an event as possible, that he may drag him back to the brick-yards. "Don't do anything rash! Be sure that you do not make a fool of yourself! Join the church at some time when there is no excitement. How many have become mentally unbalanced through religious excitement!" These are the thoughts which he injects into the mind of the awakened sinner. Thus we find that many make a profession and really seem to follow Jesus for a time, but their strength is weak, they do not persevere long, but "fall out by the way." They remind us of the little girl who fell out of bed soon after retiring. Her mother inquired how it occurred. "I went to sleep too near where I got in," said the little one. Beloved, if you halt too near where you get in you will soon fall out again.

Pharaoh's third proposition was, "Go now ye that are men and serve the Lord;" but he objects to their wives and little ones accompanying them. But Moses did not believe in "meetings for men only." He knew that a holy convocation in the wilderness without the pure, elevating presence of godly women would be impossible. Then, as now, the sisters probably had most of the piety. Perhaps Pharaoh knew that if the men trudged off alone into the desert they would soon begin to be homesick and want to go back.

When Pharaoh saw that this last ruse was of no avail he sought to prevent Israel taking with them their possessions. "Go ye, serve the Lord, only let your flocks and your herds be stayed." In the East, "the flocks and herds" are equivalent to our bank stock in the Occident. Their money was in live stock. To leave their cattle meant to leave their pocketbooks. But Moses said, "Our flocks and our herds must go, and not a hoof shall be left behind." Moses knew there would be collection boxes passed a long time before they got to Kadesh, and they must have something to contribute. There are hundreds of people who are trying to be religious who have left their pocketbooks with great carefulness within the boundaries of old Egypt. But, brother, it will take all there is of you to cross the Red Sea. If you get saved, you will have to get converted "from your hat to your heels." The Lord have mercy on our stingy souls, and teach us that "it is more blessed to give than to receive."

When Israel passed out of their Egyptian abodes they came out under blood-sprinkled lintels. God said, "When I see the blood I will pass over you." Christ's holy blood alone will protect us from the hand of the sin-avenger. Through its blessed sprinkling we are safe. Hallelujah to the slain Lamb!

CHAPTER XVIII.

ENTERING INTO CANAAN.

"And Caleb stilled the people before Moses and said, Let us go up at once and possess it, for we are well able to overcome it" (Num. xiii. 30).

When I turn to the fourth chapter of Hebrews, I find divine authority for saying that Israel's passage over Jordan into Canaan was a type of the believer's entrance into the restful experience of entire sanctification by the baptism with the Holy Ghost.

"And he brought us out from thence that he might bring us in" (Deut. vi. 23). It was God's thought and purpose that Israel should soon go from their victory on the bank of the Red Sea into "the land which he sware to their fathers." Israel made a great mistake in sending spies to spy out the land. Faith never asks questions, never investigates as to the probability of God's Word being true. If God says a land is a good land it is a good land, and faith says "Amen!" But unbelief always wants to look into the matter. The bare promise is not enough. So a committee was appointed of representative men. Doubtless cool, level-headed, calculating men were the kind desired. This committee searched out the land and found it all that God had said it was. All agreed that it was a good land, that it flowed with milk and honey, that it produced luscious grapes. But ten of the committee did not know God. They were cool and calculating, prudent and sagacious; they made estimates of the height and thickness of the walls of Jericho and of other fenced cities; they noted the people, their size and numbers, and finally came to the rational, common-sense conclusion that they could never conquer the land, although God had said, "I have given it you." Just as a man may gaze at the sun until he can see suns wherever he turns his eyes, so these men looked at giants until they saw giants everywhere. Giants filled their vision; God was eclipsed. "All the people that we saw in it were men of great stature." "And we were in our own sight as grasshoppers, and so we were in their sight." "It is a land that eateth up the inhabitants thereof." "The people be strong that dwell in the land." "Cities walled and very great." They said, "We admit that it is a 'good land,' and here is the fruit of it, grapes and pomegranates and figs, but we can never live over there. The giants will eat us up." Thousands talk in precisely this way in regard to the experience of entire sanctification into which we are brought by receiving the Holy Ghost. They admit that it is a desirable experience, but maintain that no one can live it. They say that it is very presumptuous and dangerous to profess it. "Impossible! impossible! The giants will eat us up!" Just as the ten cowardly spies failed to recognize God, so men to-day say, "We are not able." Very true; but "*God* is able."

But while the report of the committee was causing great commotion among the people, Caleb, who had "another spirit," stilled the people and said, "Let us go up at once and possess it, for we are well able to overcome it." This was a minority report.

There were two men on the Official Board who knew God and believed in holiness, and wanted to move into the land of rest and perfect love. They did not fail to see the walled cities and the giants, but they saw God as well. They knew that God was able to batter down the walls of Jericho, and that he was more than a match for all the tallest men who ever drew breath.

The unbelief of the people was very painful to Caleb and Joshua, for they rent their clothes and meanwhile stoutly asserted, "The land is an exceeding good land." "If the Lord delight in us then he will bring us into this land." "Only rebel not against the Lord, neither fear the people, for they are bread for us." When we look at our surroundings, God's

Word never seems true; when we look at ourselves we are very feeble; when we look at men or difficulties, they always seem huge, but when we look at *God* everything else sinks into insignificance. We then see the utter puerility of man and the all-surpassing greatness of God.

"But the congregation bade them stone them with stones." So it is to-day. While this is not often done literally, sharp, stony words are frequently hurled at holiness and holiness preachers. You are entirely deceived if you think you can enter the land and keep step with the Holy Ghost, and yet receive no peltings from carnal stone-throwers. If you join partnership with the blessed Paraclete and "the resolute few who dare to go through," you must expect to share the reproach that falls on the firm. The Holy Ghost is no better liked nor no more welcome than Jesus was when he was on earth. Jesus "came to his own and his own received him not." The Holy Spirit is knocking at the door of the church for admission. He is offering to carry all of our burdens, to take all our cares, to lift all the mortgages from our churches, to deliver us from all friction, worry and fret, to put us where failure is clear beyond the range of possibility, and to fill us with joy and consolation indescribable, uncontainable and unmanageable. But we are so busy with church work, with wheels and "wheels within wheels," with belts, bands, pulleys, paint, gilt, varnish, whitewash, with so many societies, so much noise, so many ceaseless activities, that we really have no time to let the Holy Ghost come in. How he would quiet things! How he would rest us! How he would still the tempests and calm the tempestuous sea!

"Let us go up at once and possess it, for we are well able to overcome it." Brother, if you will make an unconditional surrender, without the slightest reservation, of yourself, your past, your present, your future, of what you know and what you don't know, of all the unseen, unthought-of events that are to come, if you will go clear over to God, make a warranty deed of all your possessions, deliver over the papers, and turn in the keys, he will receive you and sanctify you wholly by the baptism with the Holy Ghost.

We are sometimes told that if we are greatly in the minority, we must be wrong, that if the church is almost entirely against us, we must be mistaken and misguided, and that if we have a type of piety that is not acceptable to those in ecclesiastical authority, we must be deceived. But not so! Oftentimes the smallest minorities have been in the right. "Let us go up," and "the giants" shall be "bread" for *us*. We may thus, thank God! convert all our foes into hot rolls!

CHAPTER XIX.

THE LAND AND ITS RESOURCES.

"For the land, whither thou goest in to possess it, is not as the land of Egypt, from whence ye came out, where thou sowedst thy seed and wateredst it with thy foot as a garden of herbs; but the land, whither ye go to possess it, is a land of hills and valleys and drinketh water of the rain of heaven" (Deut. xi. 10, 11).

Egypt was a flat country watered by irrigation. While the Egyptian was ditching and guttering, his land with great art and labor ("foot" is a metaphor for labor), Israel in Canaan could sit in their houses while the refreshing rains from heaven came down upon their fields. The Egyptian's attitude of body was of necessity, while cleaning out his ditches, that of humiliation, as he must look down while Israel was taught to look *up*, for their blessing. God is always *up*, and not down. He went *up* from talking with Abraham. He is always spoken of as above, on high, in heaven. We will never find God by looking down our noses. The old prophets did not mumble a few words into a handkerchief, or into their fists, but they threw back their heads, opened their mouths wide, and with upturned gaze and extended palms, cried out to God. The Lord from heaven answers such a prayer.

When we enter into Canaan we "rest from our labors as God from his." Then begins a Sabbath of the soul that lasts forever. Oh! what a relief to simply sit and drink in God's blessing and God's bounty from above! He is far "more willing to give than we are to receive."

Canaan is a "good land." It is described as a country where "fountains" and "depths" spring out of valleys and hills. Thus, whether we are on the mount of rapture and ecstasy of emotion or on the plain of faith engaged in casting out devils, in either case we will drink abundantly from flowing fountains and springs. It is in this land that we enjoy the fulfillment of this blessed promise, "And the Lord shall guide thee continually and satisfy thy soul in drought and make fat thy bones, and thou shalt be like a watered garden and like a spring of water whose waters fail not."

Among the products of "the land" we find every variety of food. "Wheat and barley," the cereals, are the necessaries of life; "figs and grapes" are some of the comforts of life, but "honey, oil and wine" are *luxuries*. Some church folks would like to make us live continually on corn-bread and barley-cake, with no knicknacks and no sweetmeats at all. But when God gets us to a place where he can trust us he furnishes not only enough for subsistence but he "loadeth us with benefits." "They shall be abundantly satisfied with the fatness of thy house, and thou shalt make them drink of the rivers of pleasure." Bless God forever! No more dry experiences, testimonies nor sermons! No more back-number blessings! Everything moist, juicy and fresh. "Oil to make the face to shine with a real heavenly luster! No more moroseness! No more blue Mondays! No more long faces nor grim graveyard countenances! No more whining nor grumbling! Hallelujah!

Oil lubricates, makes supple and prevents friction. It does away with heat and wear and tear. We were running across the State of New Jersey some time since at the rate of fifty miles an hour. The writer was very desirous of reaching New York on time, in order to catch the Fall River boat. Suddenly the train slowed down and stopped. "What is the matter?" we inquired. "A hot box," some one replied. "There it is," we said, "too high speed with too little oil." We, as churches, are running too swiftly for the oil we have with which to lubricate the bearings. Work! work! work! fret and friction! Thus it goes until a hot box stops the car and delays the passengers. On our knees and in solitary retirement with the Holy Ghost our wheels are oiled. Many are so occupied with "the Lord's" (?) work that they have no time for protracted closet prayer. In that case nothing whatever would suffer if they dropped out altogether. They had better stop and oil up. "Let thy garments be always white, and let thy head lack no ointment."

Oil will prevent our becoming censorious, harsh and critical. We are not to abuse, but rather beseech. Some have lost the sweetness of their experience fighting for the doctrine of holiness. "The servant of the Lord must not strive." It is time we had something that does not require so much apology, defense and explanation. No one has to defend the Mississippi River. They do not even have to take down the fences. She takes down her own fences when a freshet is on, and none need to fear but that she will cut her own swath. Genuine holiness will hold its own. It will conquer, overcome and be perfectly at home everywhere. When you receive the Spirit at your sanctification it is his thought and plan to care for both you and your experience.

What is sweeter than honey? Real holiness is always sweet. It is a Satanic disposition indeed that can not keep sweet when every one else is kind, polite and obliging. But the Spirit will furnish honey enough to keep you sweet when every one else is crabbed, crotchety and sour. In the land of holiness you can thrust your hand into the carcass of the most forbidding circumstance of life, take out honey and Samson-like go on your way eating sweetness.

"*Wine*, to make glad the heart of man." In "the land" we drink of God's wine, the wine of the Spirit with the beatific result that while we *feel* that we possess all things and are rich it is likewise blessedly true and real.

"Thou shalt eat bread without scarceness." Money stringencies and panics never come. Famine is unknown. We never hear the cook scraping the bottom of the flour barrel. We study no spiritual economics. "Our Father is rich!" Beloved, we have hardly tapped the inexhaustible resources of the King.

Again, in this land are "cities which we builded not," "wells which we digged not," and "vineyards which we planted not." The spoils of the enemy are for our good. The labor of the alien redounds to our blessing. Many times our opposers help us more than our friends. Satan himself is often made to work in God's chain-gang. Joseph in Egypt saw the hand of the Lord even in the evil purpose of his brethren.

In "the land" we have divine protection. "The Lord thy God careth for thee." "The eyes of the Lord are always upon it." Not only when bank-stock is going up, friends are plenty, the sky is clear, the family is well, and the balmy south wind of prosperity is blowing, but when the black, withering north wind of adversity comes down upon us, then also he is looking down and will not fail us. God's eye is never off of us in time of trial. The way we conduct ourselves in adversity proves what we are. That stoutness of heart which asserts itself when the heavens are black with disappointment and the atmosphere smells of brimstone gives us a mortgage upon God's grace and insures to us his unfailing care and watchfulness. If the devil should empty hell to overthrow us, God, if need be, would empty heaven to sustain us.

Spirituality gives correct adaptability. Paul says, "I know both how to be abased and I know how to abound." It is one thing to be abased and quite another thing to *know how* to be abased *gracefully* and *resignedly*. Many are abased frequently, but it is a source of deep mortification to them. They can not relax and go down easily. It is also a most valuable knowledge to know *how* to *abound* without being *puffed up* and elated.

In this land we do not have charge of the battle. It is not ours but God's. "Ye shall not fight in this battle." "Moreover the Lord thy God will send the hornet among them until they that are left and hide themselves from thee be destroyed." When enemies are small and hide themselves in crevices of the rocks and elude pursuit, God will dispatch the hornet and sting them out of their holes and slay them. We are without *fear* in "the land." "Thou shalt not be affrighted at them," "for the Lord thy God is among you a mighty God and terrible." "Perfect love casteth out fear." If you are troubled with it you are not in "the land."

Again, a Canaan experience is progressive. "And the Lord thy God will put out these nations before thee by little and little." In the land of purity we make the most rapid strides in holy things. Here there is an endless variety. There is nothing monotonous—hills and valleys and plains in great abundance, and these are all to be acquired by merely setting our feet upon them. All we will tread upon is ours; even to "the going down of the sun," the country is ours.

And why did God so bounteously bless us? It was certainly not because we abounded in numbers. Why did he choose us? Why did he set his love upon us? It was simply because we were willing to think more of quality and rightness than of quantity and appearance. The Lord delighteth in good quality and, when he finds it, will rain plenty upon him who possesses it.

CHAPTER XX.

SAMSON AND THE FLAW IN HIS LIFE.

"I will go out as at other times before and shake myself. And he wist not that the Lord had departed from him" (Judges xvi. 20).

Samson was a man of supernatural strength. He had strength because he was separated from the world and attached to God in covenant. This covenant, like all covenants made with God, should have been recognized as of ever-enduring obligation. So long as this covenant remained intact, so long did God stand by Samson. But although Samson was living in covenant relation with God, and although the blessing of the Lord was upon him, yet it was the gigantic mistake of his life that he never consecrated himself wholly to the Lord and received the Holy Ghost as a constant and all-powerful Indweller. "And the Spirit of the Lord began to move him *at times*" (Judges xiii. 25). This was the flaw in his life: he had power only "at times." The Holy Ghost was *with* him, but did not dwell *in* him. Christ said to his disciples before Pentecost with reference to the Spirit, "But ye know him: for he dwelleth with you and he shall be in you." Thus it was with Samson. God was *with* him *at times.* He had an enduement by spells. But "between spells" he was subject to the most awful temptations, not only from without but from within. An unlawful, inward longing for the world led him to choose a wife from the "uncircumcised Philistines." And Samson said unto his father, "Get her for me, for she is right in mine eyes." Thus there are myriads of Christians to-day who have power and victory by spells, but who during the interludes suffer most inglorious defeat. We have always maintained that it is far better for people to have salvation by spells than not to have it at all. We have no doubt that thousands who have had spells all their lives finally have a good one and die in the midst of it and go to heaven. If everyone who is "spelly" in their religious life should go to hell, heaven would be but sparsely populated. "Yet show I unto you a more excellent way." "Receive ye the Holy Ghost," and he will cure your spasmodic life.

A man once wrote to the editor of the *Boston Herald* and asked if he could give a cure for melancholy. We should like to have answered him, for we know a never-failing remedy for all moroseness, "blue Mondays," despondency, shadows and fogs.

But the time came in the life of Samson when close contact with the polluting world proved so demoralizing to his spirituality that the covenant was broken; he was robbed of his power and made the laughing-stock of the Philistines. It was at this time that he said, "I will go out as at other times before and shake myself;" but, alas! "He wist not that the Lord had departed from him." He went out and shook himself, but he had no strength to shake any one else. How many to-day, after some unholy connection with the world, go out to moral battles with the thought, "I will shake myself and be as I was before." But, alas! they have no power to make any one else shake. If all the people who have ever received the Holy Ghost in the modern holiness revival had retained him and walked and worked in his strength, this land would have felt the shock of many an earthquake. This world needs "these who turned the world upside down," and holy people only have this power.

On an iron ship the compass is up above the deck, away from all proximity to anything which would tend to make the needle unreliable. Thus the Holy Ghost would keep *us* far away from all worldly affinities.

Some years ago a ship in mid-ocean was suddenly found to be four hundred miles out of her course. It was discovered on investigation that a six-penny nail had been driven too nearly to the compass and had destroyed its trustworthiness. A very small thing, insignificant and harmless in appearance, may prevent us from going straight forward. A ship, if she be strong, can weather a very high sea so long as there is no sea in her hold, but a very small portion of the sea inside will sink the vessel in an instant. We can throw off the waves bravely and ride serenely on if the world is not in our hearts. But many lose their fire, power, and life by allowing the entrance of the world.

Some years ago, while serving a church as pastor in Smithfield, Ohio, the writer chanced to step into the house of a neighbor, where he found his little boy, four years of age, standing upon a box placed upon four glass tumblers. Our neighbor had a galvanic battery and was pouring electricity into the little fellow. They suggested that we kiss him. As we drew near, even before we touched the boy, the fire jumped from him to us. They had made him "*fire-tight*" by insulating him from the earth. So God would have us so separated from this old world that we will hold fire. Then he will fill us so full of celestial lightning that when sinners comes near us the fire will leap from us to them.

There are various ways in which men lose their power, the keen edge of their Christian experience.

1. Men lose their strength in the feverish excitement of political campaigns. It is impossible for you to become intoxicated with any worldly enthusiasm or zeal and retain your spiritual vigor. People return from political "rallies" and "caucuses" and say, "I will

go out as at other times before and shake myself." They succeed in shaking themselves, but are powerless in making wrong forces tremble. Brethren, we are "not of the world, even as He is not of the world." Suppose you and I go to England. While we are there the local John Bulls get into a squabble about some local matter of government. How much does it interest us? Does it concern us? We belong to another country. Neither are we in a true sense citizens of this earth. We are here with a message from the King, and just as soon as our work is done we shall go home.

2. Thousands lose their strength by associating with worldly men in lodges and fraternities. We have no time to spare to war against these things as worldly institutions. But we positively object to men practicing heathenish customs and serving at a Christless altar one night and then approaching a church altar in full fellowship the next. "Ye can not drink the cup of the Lord and the cup of devils; ye can not be partakers of the Lord's table and the table of devils."

3. Again men come back from county, State and World's Fairs and shake themselves and say, "I will be as before," but they are *not* as they were before. They have suffered loss.

At the risk of being severely criticized, and possibly branded as a fanatic, I feel constrained to say that these institutions are fire-stealers and juice-absorbers. During twenty years of close observation I have never known a single person who frequented these places, even for the most legitimate purposes, who did not lose the fire and juice out of his soul. A few of these run in for repairs, but thousands go on disabled all their lives. Forms without power are always revolting, but of all forms the form of *power* without the power is the most ghastly. How distressing to see a preacher trying to make up for a leakage of spiritual power by bluster, blubber, noise and bodily exercise. "And he wist not that the Lord was departed from him."

4. Women lose their spiritual force over fashion-plates. We grant you that a few people have gone to an unwarrantable extreme in harping on dress and outward adornment, but shall this be given as a reason why the great body of holiness people should give little or no attention to the extravagances in dress and jewelry which are flooding and swamping our churches? True, the Gospel strikes first at the heart, and when the heart is right and the Holy Ghost permitted to come in and is given right of way, he will regulate everything in outward as well as inward life. But he will not go contrary to the Word. He guides according to his written Bible. Thousands grieve the Spirit by failing to listen to his voice in this matter.

Many, who have laid off their jewelry and adorned themselves in modest apparel under the clear conviction of the Spirit, have come to disregard this conviction and again trigged themselves out in the trappings of the world. We have been astonished, even in holiness and Christian Alliance camps and conventions, to see the dead birds, rag flowers, Pittsburg glass, and cheap paint so lavishly in evidence. Oh, for the *heavenly* luster from above!

5. Another leakage of power is due to questionable reading. This pouring over the newspapers, reading the world's gossip by the wholesale, perusing unclean divorce cases and murders, enervates and vitiates the soul. Do you suppose that you can permit the devil to empty his scavenger wagons into your sitting-room and onto your center-table, and yet you yourself or your family remain clean or retain your spiritual power? Even much that is called "good reading," scientific reading of a very high type, may crowd out the Word and prove very damaging.

You shun as a nest of vipers all impure and degrading associations on the street. You will not permit your children to come under the influence of the vile and vulgar in social life; but in your library, perhaps, your children meet and are introduced to the vilest of souls portrayed with print on paper. It is often *here* that they come in contact with so-called "heroes" and "heroines," who speak vulgarities and blasphemies and ridicule morality and religion. Who dares to denounce the characters in literature who walk with brazen effrontery before the receptive eyes of our pure youth? Nude statues and obscene paintings in our college chapels and university halls, masking under the title of "works of fine art," are not only demoralizing in their effects upon society, but are damning multitudes of souls in hell.

6. Gossip, or light, chaffy talk, is another means of neutralizing this heavenly power. Oh, the twaddle and petty conversation of society in these days! It is not confined to women's tea parties. Some of the greatest gossips we have ever seen were men. The table and fireside talk of many a home is most damaging. Many parents criticize the minister, the sermon, the neighbors, everybody and everything, until their children lose confidence in all goodness and all sanctity and drop into infidel's hells. Your conversation in your home has been such as to destroy the faith and fidelity of your sons and daughters. You have let them slip through your fingers into cesspools of iniquity, and now you come to the evangelist and beg him to pray them out. It is not uncommon for parents to confess to us that they have lost their influence over their children. What a disgrace! What a *crime*, the effects of which will be as lasting as eternity.

Ordinarily we talk too much. "In the multitude of words there wanteth not sin." "The tongue of the just is as choice silver." "The mouth of the just bringeth forth wisdom." "The lips of the righteous know what is acceptable."

CHAPTER XXI.

POWER ABOVE THE POWER OF THE ENEMY.

"Behold, I have given you power above all the power of the enemy." "Greater is He that is in you than he that is in the world."

Men are in fearful earnest in our modern times to succeed in everything but in salvation. But thousands who will not tolerate failure in secular things complacently submit to most inglorious defeat in spiritual conflicts.

Those who receive and rely upon the Holy Ghost are never defeated. Failure is impossible with him. He will never send you on a fool's errand. You will never make a "trial" trip nor preach a "trial" sermon. There is no lottery, no uncertainty in the life of the sanctified, Holy Ghost baptized man. There are many who enter into Christian work to-day as an experiment. We as boys spit on chips and threw them into the air with the question, "Wet or dry?" In a similiar chance game the church often engages. A church will send for an evangelist and enter upon a series of meetings with great misgivings as to whether they will be a success or not. If the people knew the Holy Ghost, defeat would not only never be experienced but never even thought of. Some ministers enter the pulpit with a feeling of doubt as to whether they are going to have liberty in preaching or not. But, thank God, with those who are acquainted with the blessed Holy Ghost, bondage is never known. We *have* the victory even before we enter upon the engagement. God's Word is settled forever in heaven. The battle is not ours but God's.

> "Before the battle lines are spread,
> Before the boasting foe is dead,
> I win the fight though not begun,
> I 'll trust and shout, still marching on.
>
> "Why should I ask a sign from God?
> Can I not trust the precious blood?
> Strong in his Word I meet the foe,
> And, shouting, win without a blow."

Jehovah pays all the bills, takes care of the property, does all the work, and then permits us to rejoice as heartily as if we did it all ourselves. Our failure is always the result of not depending absolutely upon him. You may be ever so orthodox and startle the world with your eloquence; you may preach logical, unanswerable sermons; you may be a great rhetorician; you may lead an amiable, commendable Christian life, but without "the Holy Ghost sent down from heaven," your words will fall flat on the congregation, while an uncouth, grotesque, awkward fellow who murders the King's English, if he have the Holy Ghost upon and in him, will win victory and a multitude of souls.

We are too awfully proper. Regularity and formality is stifling the spiritual life of the church. We are starched before we are washed, and the dirt is "set" in the grain of the fabric. When the freshet of the Pentecostal out-pouring dashes into our souls it breaks up our cast-iron respectability and enriches the Delta with an overflow. The Spirit will help us down from our stilts, break us up and break us down, and make us so supple and adjustible that he can use us anywhere at any time. He will not pin himself to our programmes. He does not work in human harness, neither does he repeat or duplicate his work. In the average Protestant church "he who runs may read" precisely what will occur in the Sabbath morning service at least four days before the thing comes off. All is "cut and dried," and no margin is left for the Holy Ghost.

The Spirit will also give us wisdom so that we may avoid loading our guns with blank cartridges, or even with fine bird shot. If you will inspect the charge thrown from many a pulpit gun, you will not be astonished at the size of the game taken. Pewee shot will kill nothing but pewees. The Holy Ghost would roll the artillery of heaven into our pulpits and plant the "Swamp Eagle" behind the desk loaded to the muzzle with grape and canister. God wants men who are not afraid to bombard the battlements of hell. God is our defence. "The conies are but a feeble folk, yet make they their houses in the rocks."

The coming of the Holy Ghost clarifies our vision so that we "see the King in his beauty." He who sits on the throne fills all the horizon of our view, eclipsing all lesser lights and deluging us with luminous glory. We see a "land that is very far off." The spiritual eye is more piercing and more acute than the eye of reason.

From Lick Observatory they see myriads of worlds that the unaided natural eye will never discern, but we who are spiritually discerning see far beyond all these worlds, on, up, up to the throne of God and Jesus sitting at the right hand. We can see the burnished walls and glittering towers and shining gates and streets of gold. We can hear the music of the angels, Yea, we can pierce with our anointed eyes even into the council chambers of the King. Glory!

CHAPTER XXII.

COMPROMISE.

This is an age of expediency, policy and compromise.

There never was a time in the history of the world when there was more need of moral heroes and heroines than to-day. Probably there never was a time when there was so many moral cowards in proportion to the number of professed Christians. This is preeminently an ease-loving, time-serving, compromising generation. In politics, men mind only the crack of the whip of their political boss.

In the commercial world, who dares to speak out against questionable practices and business trickery?

In social circles, men and women are afraid to hazard their reputation for the sake of principle.

In the religious world, there are very few who are not in bondage to a pope or ecclesiastical boss. In nearly every congregation may be found a "weighty," "influential" man, who as really rules in all church matters as if he was appointed for that purpose.

Few there are who dare protest against this religious popery. Our fathers had convictions born of certainty, and courage sufficient to enable them to stand *by* their convictions. You might take George Fox's head off, but he would not take his hat off if he had a conviction that he ought to keep it on. We hear a great deal of talk, cheap talk, about *unity* and *conciliation*, but how little is said about principle and loyalty to the leadings of the Holy Ghost. There is a great hue and cry about loyalty to the church. This is right only so long as the church is right.

What if Martin Luther, George Fox or John Wesley had been loyal to all the edicts of the church? We forget that loyalty to the society or organization *may* mean disloyalty to God. Every true disciple is loyal first to the will of God. Other things may come second, but this must be first. Unity must be upon a good foundation. The kingdom of heaven is first pure, then peaceable.

We see on every hand the dire effects of this spirit of compromise. The result is, without exception, in every case deplorable. It produces a very low type of spirituality. No man, or set of men, can be deeply spiritual while they cater to the opinions and goodwill of others, and lean on human dependencies. The Church is stocked with putty men. We need spinal columns; tow-strings can never do the work of backbones. Compromise produces overgrown babies instead of soldiers, weaklings instead of stalwarts, pigmies and dwarfs instead of Titans. This world is radical as hell itself. Our holy Christianity is radical, aggressive and uncompromising. Our fathers were not afraid to attack sin in high places. They did not hesitate to oppose organized ecclesiastical authority. They went boldly into the "steeple-houses" and denounced worldliness and error. They were inflexible and incorrigible. Mary Dyre went back to Boston, not because she was wanted, but because she was needed. This sweet, sickish, sentimental gush about "love and unity" which composes the stock in trade of a great many religious tongue-waggers is producing a race of cringing, sensitive, puny, delicate Christians, who wilt and curl up under a hot sun. Genuine love is not only sweet but faithful. So far as unity is concerned it may be said that harmony and quietness do not argue spirituality. There is unity in a cemetery. There is no quarreling, no difference of opinion, no one is offended or hurt by the action of any of the inmates. We know congregations where perfect unity prevails, and yet they are as dead to the real work of Jesus Christ in the earth as are the frozen corpses in a graveyard. The love of God shed abroad in the human heart by the Holy Ghost is a faithful love that will not permit men to slip through our fingers into hell without being warned to flee from the wrath to come. It will deplore and denounce all sin, and rebuke worldliness, compromise and truckling, wherever found. The unity that is needed in these times is a combined force of men and women "who love nothing but God, and hate nothing but sin," and who are not only able to resist the artillery of hell, but who are not afraid to bombard the very gates of pitted evil. Hell is filling at an alarming rate, all for the want of an uncompromising, faithful ministry. The spirit of compromise is manifest, we regret to say, in many of our ministers who are in such bondage to men of means or of supposed superior intelligence, that they dare not preach a full gospel. They are afraid they will lose their "bread and butter." It would have been difficult, a few years ago, to have convinced us that this state of affairs would ever prevail among the Friends. But, alas! it is upon us. Pastors are already confessing that they do not *dare* preach all their convictions of the truth, else they will lose their support.

We say a great deal about popery and priestcraft, about the American pew being in bondage to the American pulpit; but our immediate danger is that the pulpit is getting in bondage to the pew. Oh, that we might let the Lord strike off every shackle and set us scot-free, that we may preach the *Word* and declare the whole truth. Before the simple but fiery preaching of the cross of Christ, worldliness, cowardice and compromise will melt away, legions of devils will turn pale and gnash their teeth in impotent rage, and the Church will shine with celestial luster.

The only possible cure for compromise is Pentecost. Fire from heaven will burn out all fear and make us good soldiers, ready for a dreary march through the desert, heavy work in the trenches, live on scant rations or anything that God may ordain. If need be the Pentecostal soldier will make a bridge of his dead body, over which his comrades may march to victory.

CHAPTER XXIII.

THE FULLNESS OF GOD.

"That ye might be filled with all the fullness of God" (Eph. iii. 19). Paul was a man of profound character, deep spirituality, and unusual breadth of soul. He was often filled, as many references to his epistles would show, if we had space to adduce them, with an intense longing that the saints might be brought into "the fullness of the blessing of the Gospel of Christ." He knew that this would give them such a view of the magnitude of their inheritance in Christ that their divorcement from the paltry things of this earth and their attachment to things eternal would be forever perpetuated. Christ says, "I am come that they might have *life* and that they might have it more abundantly." We receive divine life when we are born from above, in regeneration, but we do not get the fullness of life until we are sanctified wholly by the baptism with the Holy Ghost. One may have life and be sick and even in the hospital. And thousands of people can say with truth that they have spiritual life and yet they are sickly, dwarfish, undersize, utterly incapacitated for a soldier's service in the open field. Many churches are nothing but hospitals, while God's picture of his church is "an army with banners."

Every Christian received the *love* of God into his heart when he was converted. This love is not perfected then, but it is supreme and predominant. If you had an enemy when you were regenerated, you forgave him frankly and gladly. More than this, you positively *loved* him. It does not take entire sanctification to set you right with men. Genuine conversion will do that much. But the love of the *merely* regenerate (we use the word "merely" in this connection in an accommodated sense, and not as comparing the work of regeneration with that of sanctification) is by universal testimony more or less mixed. It is often vacillating and adulterated and mingled with a gross alloy. But the fullness of love brought into the soul at Pentecost is constant, unchanging and steady. The world is languishing and dying for the want of this love.

Every child of God has *joy*. He received joy when he was born of the Spirit. Every real convert is made joyful and glad by the work of the Lord in his heart. Some express it in one way and some in another, but all have it. Not only do all Christians have joy at first, but they have it afterwards, by spells at least. But it can not be assumed that all Christians have *constant* joy. Not every one of God's dear children obeys literally the positive command of the Apostle, "Rejoice evermore." To assert that none are Christians except those who "rejoice evermore," is to un-Christianize nine-tenths of our church membership, and that is not Scriptural. But there is a fuller grace and a more luscious experience that will fulfill in the hearts of every one of us the injunction of Paul. To "rejoice evermore," if you are a farmer, means to *rejoice* when the hogs get into the corn, when your neighbor's stock breaks through the fence and tramples your grain and ruins your young fruit-trees. If you are a teamster, it means to *rejoice* when your horse balks and will not pull a pound. Instead of whipping and scolding you just stop and hold a miniature camp-meeting, with singing and shouting and all the rest of the things that usually go with holiness camp-meetings, and the horse will grow ashamed of himself and move on beautifully. If you are a mechanic, it means to *rejoice* when you hit the wrong nail. Instead of blurting semi-profanity you say, "Hallelujah!" If you are a country house-wife, it means to *rejoice* when the clothes-line breaks and lets your white linen into the mud, or when the bread burns and the baby cries and you are half sick, and the devil piles up before you the long list of household duties with washing and ironing and baking and mending and a hundred other things all included. Then *you* stop just a moment and hold your camp-meeting. If on the other hand you, brother, are a husband and come home for your dinner, anxious to get back to your work and you find "the washing not out," the baby squalling and the dinner half an hour late, then just raise both hands and shout, "Glory to God!" Instead of storming around and muttering about "the injustice of a tired man, hungry as a bear, waiting for a bite to eat at noon when dinner ought to be ready," and finally subsiding behind a newspaper or a book, while your wife hurries up the dinner, you jump out of your easy chair and help that poor, tired, half-sick wife of yours. Take that baby out of the crib and dry his tears and say, "Praise the Lord! It's all right, wife; I am awfully sorry you have had such a trying time this morning, but it will be better this afternoon." Then you place the chairs to the table and fill the ice pitcher and, when you sit down to eat, thank God for the food, burnt bread and all! Bless you, this "rejoicing evermore" is the most practical thing in existence. If you are a merchant, *you* need to "rejoice evermore." There are Christian merchants who will stand and see their homes go up in flames and smoke and rush to the Lord for sustaining grace to say, "The Lord giveth and the Lord taketh away. Blessed be the name of the Lord," who, if their over-worked bookkeeper comes to her work five minutes late Monday morning, will fly into a passion and sin against God. If you are a woman with servants, the Apostle meant you when he said, "Rejoice evermore." This you can do when the servants fail to perform your wishes, or when you have had four cooks in three weeks and every one unsatisfactory. If you are a servant, you can smile and rejoice in your heart when your mistress is crotchety and crabbed and hard to please. This fullness of joy comes only in the experience of entire sanctification when the Holy Ghost comes to abide in the heart. Take, for instance, that command, "In everything give thanks, for this is the will of God in Christ Jesus, concerning you." Every real Christian is thankful at times, but not every Christian is thankful in *everything*.

There is a fullness of prayer. We are distinctly commanded to "pray without ceasing." Now every Christian prays, but do all "pray without ceasing"? By no means. But it is possible to be ever in a prayerful state of mind, to live continually in an element of prayer. Christians who have not received the Holy Ghost have hindrances to prayer which are purely subjective and internal. They do not always *feel* like praying. But a sanctified man can pray day or night, rain or shine. He always has his prayer-book ready. You may rout him out at midnight, but you can not surprise him in a state of mind unready for a prayer-meeting. This "fullness of God," which is the theme of the present chapter, furnishes the *spontaneous* elements in the Gospel. Too few Christians get *full.* Too much in these days is by constraint and effort. Too much is formal, mechanical, worked-up and pumped-up. The spontaneity of the Gospel is rarely known. But Christianity is not a product of coercion, nor conscious striving, nor automatic, machine-like action. It springs from a life-center and lives as the flower lives, beautifully, easily, naturally, normally. The "fullness of God" gives an *establishment* that nothing else will produce. That majestic tree, towering in the air, covered with foliage and loaded with fruit, has roots of proportional strength and depth. It would not do for it to grow tall if it did not grow deep. At times this tree bows and sways and bends in the tempest, until it seems as if it must go down, and then it straightens back to its place, only to lock in once more with the tornado, swinging and groaning and bending, but when the storm is completely past, it comes proudly back to its place with a richer green and a tougher fiber than before.

The Holy Ghost gives us roots. Just as the oak takes hold of the rocks and springs far down within the earth, so our spiritual roots take hold of the Rock of Ages and the fountains of living waters, so that we can withstand the wildest gale that breaks upon our heads. We are only the better for the storm. The floating ship turns out for the embedded rock. If we are not established in our convictions and experiences, when we meet positive characters who are filled with error, we will turn out for them. But if we are *rooted, grounded* and *established*, they will turn out for us. A man who has received the Holy Ghost will never measure his faith in a calm, but rather in the storm. Paul stood on the deck of that old Roman corn ship, with her sails and masts all torn away, and said, calmly, "Be of good cheer, for I believe God that it shall be even as it was told me." That was a good time for Paul to take an inventory of the faith in stock. He did so, and found himself well supplied.

Beloved, do n't measure your spirituality at high-tide. What Paul had in that storm would stay with him. When finances have been low, or friends have failed, or bitter reverses have struck us, and seemed almost to over-topple us, my dear wife has said brightly, "What we have now we have surely. What we have now will stay with us forever." If you take account of stock at camp-meeting or on the mount of holy ecstasy, you may experience shrinkage, but if you throw out the plumb-line at low-tide you will get a correct estimate. The grace which you possess in severe trial is *bona fide.* May God help us to empty ourselves of all things un-Christlike and receive the fullness of God.

CHAPTER XIV.

EXPERIENCE.

Frugally brought up on a Western farm by godly Quaker parents, my early youth was well preserved from close contact with this evil world. Its ways, customs and maxims were almost wholly unknown to us. Though our meetings for divine worship were frequently held in profound and unbroken silence, I was rarely absent from my accustomed place by my father's side in the quaint, severely plain, unpainted old meeting-house. It was not uncommon for six or seven hundred people, most of them Friends, to assemble at our regular First-day morning meeting. The plank benches were hard, the backs straight and uncomfortable, and my feet did not touch the floor by many inches. Added to this was the rigorous rule of keeping perfectly still, and yet I have some most blessed memories of those early days. I devoutly thank God that, in the matter of church attendance, my youthful education was not neglected.

But I regret to record that early in my teens I threw off the lines of restraint, and for several years a wild, impetuous, evil spirit carried me into sin. It was under the faithful, fiery ministry of the now sainted Calvin W. Pritchard, in third month, 1873, that I was put under deep and pungent conviction for sin, and gloriously converted to God.

The "anxious seat," or "penitent form," was not then used in our meetings, but at the close of a sermon preached "with the Holy Ghost sent down from heaven," all were requested to stand who desired the prayers of God's people. To the utter astonishment of a large congregation, almost all of which knew me personally, I arose to my feet. I had not at that time the most remote idea of ever being converted. In fact, I had no thought that it was possible for me to to be saved. I remember distinctly of saying to myself, "I will give them a good subject for them to try their hand on." No further request was made, and no one spoke to me about the step I had taken.

To a similar invitation the next evening I stood up, more because I had done so the night before than anything else. But now I very soon began "to feel serious," and when on First-day night a different call was made and all were asked to arise who sincerely desired to become Christians, in company with a number of others, I promptly responded. Nothing more was said to me, either publicly or privately, but the dear Holy Spirit suggested to me that I attend the day meeting on Second-day morning.

9

As I entered the meeting-house yard a neighbor said: "Will thee come and sit with me?" and without waiting for an answer he led the way to a seat much further forward than I had been accustomed to occupy since I was a boy. I had not long been seated when the Spirit fell upon the congregation, and the meeting proved to be one of testimony and confession. When the meeting was well under way a strange power came over me, and I rose to my feet and confessed that I was an awful sinner. I was not on my feet thirty seconds, but I sat down a saint! It seemed as if all heaven dropped into my soul. Up to that time I had not attempted to pray. I had not shed a tear. Now my eyes were fountains, and wept like rain. The complexion of everything changed. Every blade of grass, every drop of water and every bird of forest and field, seemed to dance with delight.

I conferred not with flesh and blood, but under the immediate and perceptible guidance of the Spirit, I went out into school-houses and churches, and held meetings in various parts of Indiana and Ohio. Hundreds were converted, for great and lasting revivals came down upon the people. Almost before I had considered what my calling was, the meeting of which I was a member had acknowledged my gift and recorded me a minister of the Gospel of Christ.

But it was not long before I found the motions of

evil within me. I was not a little surprised to discover that there was a sin-principle remaining in my breast, which mocked, persecuted and threatened the new life. It required great devotion and much prayer and watching to remain in victory. I had seasons of great depression of spirit, and sometimes suffered temporary defeat. At other times I would ascend to mounts of rapture and ecstasy. I know now that I was led to profess sanctification when I did not possess that blessed grace. I said, "I have taken Christ as my Sanctifier. I just claim it by faith. The altar sanctifies the gift," etc. But I had never had a real funeral. Under ordinary preaching I felt fairly comfortable, and could stand to all the tests put to the congregation. But under the search-light of the ministry of such men as David B. Updegraff or Dr. Dougan Clark, I would feel keenly conscious of a shortage in my experience. Again and again have I rushed from the meeting into the woods or open country, by day or by night, to weep and cry to God for hours. I really reached a state of conviction, even after I had preached for years, when the wretchedness and anguish of my heart was often inconceivable. My suffering under conviction for inbred sin greatly surpassed anything I endured when an awakened sinner. I had been in the ministry for ten years and, incongruous and presumptuous as it may seem, I had dreamed of places of prominence and honor in my church. To give up my reputation and renounce my ambition for place, and die out completely to what might be said or thought about me, seemed more than I could possibly do. But the Holy Ghost had "harpooned" me, and I found no rest, day nor night, until I gave up entirely. I went on my face before God and lay prostrate before him, crying for deliverance from the "old man." I longed for human sympathy. I remembered ministers whom I thought could help me, but no help came. It was the darkest day I ever saw. After hours of agony I began to be filled with a sense of sinking, sinking, and it seemed as if I was dying. Then I began to say, "Yes," to the Lord, "Yes! Yes! Amen! Amen! Amen!" The past, present and future, all the known and all the unknown, my reputation, my all, went into God's lap. I gladly consented to be deposed from the ministry. One of the things that the Holy Ghost brought before me at that time was my future attitude toward the distinctive views of our Society—the Quaker Church. Would I follow Him if it led me contrary to my previous religious teaching? I little knew then what was implied or what it would cost me to make this consecration, but I said "Yes." I "died hard," but I "died sure." At last there began to creep into my soul a tranquil feeling, a holy hush, a death-like stillness, a sweet, placid "*second* rest." I had let go, and He had embraced me in His arms. Eight hours later the conscious filling came, and from that hour I had convictions of certainty. "The old man" was "put off," "the body of sin" was "destroyed," "the old leaven" was "purged out," "the flesh" was "cut away," "the son of the bondwoman" was "excommunicated," "the carnal mind" was "crucified," and I was dead indeed unto sin. HE did it. No credit belongs to me. The Holy Ghost came in, cleansed the temple, spread the table, and I took supper with the Father, Son and Holy Ghost, that very day. He settled all my difficulties, expelled all my doubts, metamorphosed my duties into delights, dazzled my head with glory and filled my heart with dancing.

I am deeply regretful that for years after this I sometimes grieved the Spirit by permitting myself to worry, thus allowing friction and worry to come in. Instead of relying entirely upon the Holy Ghost, I was betrayed into a rigid, severe life. I was marvelously preserved from sin, but lacked the sweetness and juice and absolute freedom from care that the Holy Ghost wishes to maintain in His wholly sanctified people. I lost much of the kernel of the *experience* fighting for the *doctrine*.

A few years since the Holy Ghost taught me more perfectly how to cast and keep all my care on Him, for "He careth for you." I took my hands off of men, whether friends or foes; off of my experience, my circumstances, my interests, myself; off of everybody and everything. I am leaning upon the arm of my Beloved. No more irksome tasks, no more "toiling and rowing," no more worry, fret or friction! Never a "hot box!" He is no more "*Baali*" (Master or Lord), but "*Ishi*" (my husband). Hallelujah!

THE END.

Colportage

Holiness Booklets.

Pentecostal.

Loyal. Evangelical.

Salvation Papers. S. A. KEEN. 10c.
The Better Way. Abridged. B. CARRADINE. 10c.
The Double Cure. M. W. KNAPP. 10c.
Gifts and Graces. W. B. GODBEY. 10c.
Victory. W. B. GODBEY. 10c.
Sins Versus Infirmities. B. S. TAYLOR. 10c.
Canaanites. B. S. TAYLOR. 10c.
Salvation Melodies. From "Tears and Triumphs." 10c.
Pentecostal Sanctification. S. A. KEEN. 10c.
Holy Land. W. B. GODBEY. 10c.
Pentecostal Church. Abridged. S. C. REES. 10c.
Pentecostal Preachers. From "Bolts." M. W. KNAPP. 10c.
Sanctified Life. Abridged. B. CARRADINE. 10c.
Pentecostal Light. A. M. HILLS. 10c.
Romanism to Pentecost. J. S. DEMPSTER. 10c.
Types of the Spirit. G. D. WATSON. 10c.
Spirit of Jesus. E. H. DASHIELL. 10c.
Pentecostal Wine from "Bible Grapes." By CARRADINE, REES, and others. 140 pp. 20c.
Impressions. M. W. KNAPP. 140 pp. 20c.
Life of Madam Guyon. Introduction by ABBIE C. MORROW. 20c.
River of Death. M. W. KNAPP. (For the young.) 15c.
Morning Glories. ABBIE C. MORROW. (For the Young.) 20c.
Flashes from Lightning Bolts. M. W. KNAPP. 15c.
Burning Coals. From Fire from Heaven. SETH C. REES. 10c.
Joy and Rejoicing. Pentecostal Bible Readings. ABBIE C. MORROW and C. W. MCCROSSAN. 10c.
The Heart-Cry of Jesus. BYRON J. REES. 10c.
Pentecostal Messengers. SETH C. REES, B. CARRADINE, W. B. GODBEY, A. M. HILLS, and others. 10c.
Sparks from Revival Kindlings. M. W. KNAPP. 10c.
Light and Shadow. Christian Science Exposed. FORREST W. BEERS. 15c.
Jesus Only. Year Book. BY GODBEY, CARRADINE, REES and others. 25c.
Pentecostal Aggressiveness. M. W. KNAPP. 10c.
Paul to the Thessalonians. W. B. GODBEY. 10c.
Out of Egypt into Canaan. (Reprint.) M. W. KNAPP. 25c.
Food for Lambs. Abridged. A. M. HILLS. 10c.
Pentecostal Kernels. D. B. UPDEGRAFF. 10c.
The Holy Nation. R. L. SELLE. 10c.
Whosoever Gospel. A. M. HILLS. 10c.
Trumpet Calls to the Unconverted. BYRON J. REES. 20c.
Electric Shocks from Pentecostal Batteries. Food and Fire from Salvation Park Camp-meeting. 20c.
The Return of Jesus. W. B. GODBEY and SETH C. REES. 10c.
Soul Laws in Sexual, Social, and Spiritual Life. F. S. HEATH. 10c.
Life of Faith Through Geo. Muller. ABBIE C. MORROW. 20c.
Modern Miracles. H. T. DAVIS. 25c.

Any number will be sent on receipt of price. Special rates by the quantity.

One dollar and forty cents' worth of the above **not prepaid** and GOD'S REVIVALIST for one year, only $2.00.

AGENTS AND BOOK EVANGELISTS WANTED WHEREVER ENGLISH IS SPOKEN.

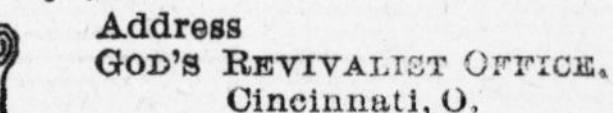

Address
GOD'S REVIVALIST OFFICE,
Cincinnati, O.